I0142540

TASTEFUL DIVERSITY

STORIES OUR FOODS TELL

Publishing for Community

2019

EDITOR
Michael Vander Weele

COVER & LAYOUT
Schuyler Roozeboom

TASTEFUL DIVERSITY
ISBN 978-0-578-50499-5
ISBN 978-0-578-50500-8 ebook

Copyright © 2019 Publishing for Community
All rights reserved.

TABLE OF CONTENTS

FOREWORD

"Getting to Know Us: The Story of Our Foods" seemed like a good first assignment for a writing course. We could hypothesize a small book of essays for friends and family. We could learn as much as we could from Nina Mukerjee Fursteneau, an Indian-American writing somewhere along the Missouri-Kansas border about her access to Indian foods, family, and culture. We could write well about things we knew. Get to know each other better. Enjoy our diversity. (*See the original assignment in the Appendix.*)

When the essays came in, I was stunned. We not only had three Korean young women in the room, but Shinhye was from Cambodia and Jessie from Peru. Naomi was only one generation removed from Eretria & Ethiopia, Paulette two generations from Mexico, Andrea two generations from the Philippines. Other students had somewhat more distant cultural connections to Ireland, Lithuania, the Netherlands, Germany, Italy. Parents, grandparents, uncles, aunts, siblings, and friends came into their stories. As with Fursteneau, so too with us, stories about food could become stories about family and culture.

And who knew the foods would range from beer brats and OJ banana bread muffins to *kugelis* and *himbasha*, to lumpia and *Young Yang Bab*, to *Ddok-Bok-Gi* and *mole poblano*, to *Janchi Guksu* and Keating (Irish) potatoes! The foods, family histories, and cultural insights seemed too good to keep to ourselves. They were also good reminders that we image God better together than separately. We hope you enjoy this sampling, collected over the four-year period from 2015 to 2019. Maybe you'll imagine your story better, too.

Michael Vander Weele

AMERICAN LUMPIA: FILIPINO EGG ROLL

BY Andrea Taylor

The San Francisco Bay area is my home—a center of diversity and culture in every way, especially food. Because we live in a large city near a port, finding food from my mother's home country, the Philippines, was never an obstacle.

My mother's go-to place for food from the Philippines was the International Market. There we could find anything Asian, including anything Filipino. My mother usually bought ingredients for lumpia, our family's personalized culinary specialty. She could buy the necessary items in bulk, especially the eggroll wrappers, which were hard to find in regular supermarkets. As we entered the International Market, we would see at eye-level the Hindu idols surrounded by fruit sacrifices. I always wondered why people would give inanimate objects perfectly good fruit. We would snake around the alcohol stand to the produce section, where we found vegetables that Lola, my grandma from the Philippines, liked to put in soups. We also found the carrots and onions needed for our lumpia there. Nearer the back, we would watch the fresh fish and crabs swim in their tanks before picking up oyster sauce and water chestnuts from the canned food section. During our shopping excursions, my mother would often run into another Filipino and strike up a conversation in Tagalog, the national language of the Philippines. She always hoped that this person would be from her region so that they could speak with her in a Southern Philippines dialect. There was always a little disappointment when my mother found out that they were not from her island, but she would still be pleasant. Occasionally, walking down an aisle, we would see someone my mom knew, and the two women would stop for hours to get caught up with each other. Hours later, my mom might invite them to come over to our house for dinner and have some lumpia. She was seldom refused.

When I think of lumpia being made at my house, I hold these memories close: the sound of the food processor intertwined with the squish and squash of meat enfolding the remainder of the ingredients; the sight of my mother measuring each ingredient with her experienced eyes; my Lola leaning over a large tub full of ground pork and beef, using the force of her entire body and the strength of her hands to push the ingredients into the crevices of the meat; the melodic sounds of Mommy and Lola chattering back and forth in their dialect, discussing the welfare of my cousins, aunties, and uncles across the seas back home in the Philippine Islands. When Lola is ready to begin wrapping the meat, she asks me to slowly and carefully separate the thin egg roll wrappers from their stack. Once the meat and vegetables are wrapped just right, some of the lumpia will go into the freezer to be sold or given away and some will be set aside for our dinner that night.

To complete our meal, we would prepare rice in the ever-present rice cooker and our special sauce concoction to go with the lumpia and rice. I would be sent outside to grab the yellowest lemons I could find from the tree in the backyard, lifting up my shirt to carry them back inside again. We would cut and squeeze the lemons and put an even proportion of soy sauce and lemon juice inside a shallow bowl. If the lemon tree was ever bare, we had to resort to vinegar, but it was never the same without the distinctive taste of the lemon zest dancing together with the other flavors in my mouth. When all was done, I would call my brothers and my dad to the table and we would all eat lumpia together.

Filipino lumpia finds its origins deep in Asia, with its roots traceable to China and Guam. Traditional lumpia is only a couple inches long and about half an inch in diameter. They are more wrapper than meat and very crunchy. When my mother moved here to America and married my father, she made lumpia the way that it was made in the Philippines. My father would always say, "Americans like meat! We should make lumpia fatter and longer." Slowly the lumpia began to grow longer, increasing from two inches to seven inches long. They also grew rounder, plumping from half an inch in diameter to one and a half inches. Mommy invented her own version of lumpia and named it "American lumpia." American lumpia became very popular in both church and community.

The Taylor family is known for our special American lumpia. Every year, my mother sells her lumpia to help raise money for summer camp for the children of my church. We make and freeze lumpia in mass quantities beforehand and then sell them by the dozen: $12 per dozen for packages of frozen and $15 per dozen for pre-fried. We set up a table in the foyer so people can smell the aroma as they walk in and out of church. Everybody we know loves them. They often consult with Mom since she knows how to cook them to the perfect crispness. This food has become part of our identity as a family. It has also helped connect us with our church family and community. American lumpia is a gift from my family's kitchen to the kitchen of those we love.

• • •

AMERICAN LUMPIA

INGREDIENTS (ESTIMATED PROPORTIONS)

1 lb ground pork or beef

1 can water chestnuts

1 cup ground carrots

½ cup sliced green onions

3–5 eggs

¼ cup oyster sauce

¼ cup soy sauce

2–3 Tbsps garlic

1–2 Tbsps ground pepper

1 package wrappers

DIRECTIONS

1. Grind chestnuts and carrots.
2. Chop green onions.
3. Mix all ingredients with meat of choice.
4. Wrap **1–2 Tbsps** of meat for every wrapper.
5. Deep fry until golden brown.

REWORKING THE DOUGH

BY Kate Meyrick

My dad calls us "mutts." We're Europeans, no doubt, but after five generations in Chicago, the past is so far behind us that the heritage of towns, countries, and family names in Europe are now blended into short lists of great-great grandparents, stacks of unlabeled photographs, and stories about life in London, in Bohemia, in Germany, and in Dublin (though no one can speak to their truth or accuracy). These histories are sometimes recollected during the times we are all gathered for the holidays: the times we cook, eat, sleep, and cook again. Papa and Sweetie's house is in the southern suburbs, and it's in that cramped, Christmas-laden kitchen where we putz around, talking loudly, consuming the pickle plate, never forgetting to tell the same stories we told the holiday before. This is where and how I learned we were a mish-mash.

I can hear my grandmother's thick, nasal laugh and my grandfather's quiet, soft-spoken conversations about what life used to be like—with a Pepsi in one hand, reading glasses in another. Gramma Sweetie has every cabinet open, per usual, making a simple walk-through a treacherous escapade. The ham sizzles in the oven, luscious with brown sugar, spicy with pepper, tangy with pineapple. Papa and I debate whether his grandfather came through Ellis

Island. The potatoes are laden with thick yellow butter, but the cream cheese and sour cream is what makes them so wonderfully wrought with calories. Papa tells a story of when his father played piano in a nightclub in Orlando in the 40s. Aunt Karen finishes putting together the sweet potato casserole: crunchy on top, smooth in the middle, chock-full of pecans, just the way we all prefer.

Distracted by my grandfather's tales, I pound the crust for the apple pie. "You can't handle it too much, sweetie, or it won't be tender. It doesn't matter if it's not perfect," Gramma says as I roll up the dough again.

My mother tells me, often with a laugh, that having dinner with my father's family for the first time opened her eyes to how meat could be savory and soup could be seasoned. Mom was English, through and through. Sure there was a bit of Irish thrown in there, and thanks to great-great-grandpa Anton a smidge of East Europe, but the steak was always well-done, the vegetables forever boiled, and the potatoes mashed so hard they stuck to the roof of one's mouth. Salad was her consolation, full of dressing in which she could dip her over-cooked beef and limply cold carrots. Dad quite literally gave her a whole new menu to explore through the cooking of his family: tacos with salsa and avocado, garlic-laden chicken cooked on the grill in the backyard, al dente spaghetti that survived the stick-test performed on the kitchen cabinets, gorgeous Polish *kolaczki* filled with jams and Nutella under a mountain of powdered sugar for dessert. The heritage of food in Chicago permeated my dad's family's holidays: corned beef and cabbage on St. Patrick's Day, *paczki* on Fat Tuesday, red chili with beans on game day, hot dogs with relish and onion and *absolutely no* ketchup on Labor Day, and large veggie and sausage pizzas from Aurelio's for any given Friday night. They didn't know where they came from. So they ate everything.

There was always something about Gramma's pies—cliché, I know, but she takes such pride in them. She crafts them ahead of time, and she plans days solely for mixing fillings and bagging them for later. She makes crusts and freezes them so she can whip one out any time we are in need for a pumpkin or apple fix. She taught me how to make them, and make them well, and know the reason why I am making them. She tells me how she adapts her mother's techniques, and sometimes changes them completely because she found a way to give it more flavor: more time in the oven, a little less water, generous with the cinnamon. I cannot say the same for the stories her husband tells me as we go through the monotony of rolling dough, spreading it on the filling, and pinching the crust. He cannot tell me how we got here, and the reason we came. He cannot tell me about his father. I only know that my Papa is nothing like my father's Papa. It's a hard history. Mostly because we simply don't know it. I think Papa and I feel a loss. We feel a bit too stretched, yet at the same time we feel mashed together.

I realize that I am re-rolling the crust for the apple pie, and Gramma intervenes. She has finished mixing the fresh Granny Smiths with sugar, water, cinnamon, nutmeg, and a tiny bit of flour. The bottom crust is already browned and ready to go, awaiting the top of the pie to be covered, pinched, and sliced. "You can't keep reworking the dough, sweetie, because the more you handle it the less flaky it will be. Trust me, it's all right if it's not perfect." She takes the rolling pin from me and with a broad, experienced motion rolls the crust, flips it over the pin, and lays it atop the golden apples. She efficiently and effortlessly pinches the edges and splits three holes in the middle. I run to the cabinet to grab three mostaccioli pastas, and sticking them into the splices, create the beloved "chimneys" that the cousins will fight over as soon as the pie comes out of the oven bubbling with sugar and sweet apple juices.

I look over at Papa, who is helping Dad carve the ham, and I realize that like every family, we are not perfect: we have a history that leaves much to be desired and we lay claim to stories that have probably been overworked. "But think of the richness, Papa," I want to tell him, "think of how we can soak up the culture of diversity around us, think about how we have adopted this city as our own… we are more Chicagoan than anything, and that is something to be proud about." I'm sure he understands this. I'm sure he's thought about it often. But I think we both love to think of what could have been or might be, just as Gramma and I both love to try a little more butter or a little less nutmeg. I know for sure that one day I will tell him—I will tell all of them—what a joy it is, not only to be a mutt, but to be a Meyrick.

. . .

APPLE PIE

CRUST INGREDIENTS

2½ **cups** all-purpose flour, plus extra for rolling

1 **cup** (**2 sticks** or **8 oz**) unsalted butter, very cold, cut into cubes

1 **tsp** salt

1 **tsp** sugar

6–8 **Tbsps** ice water

DIRECTIONS (FOR THE CRUST)

Using a hand-held, wire mixer, crumble the flour, butter, salt and sugar together, making sure to "cut" the butter and incorporate it generously. The mixture should be crumbly. A teaspoon at a time, add the ice water until the mixture *just barely* sticks together. Add too much and the dough will be tough. Split the mixture in half: one will be for the bottom crust. Refrigerate while you make the filling.

FILLING INGREDIENTS

6 **cups** thinly sliced, peeled apples (**6** medium)

¾ **cup** sugar

2 **Tbsps** all-purpose flour

¾ **tsp** ground cinnamon

¼ **tsp** salt

⅛ **tsp** ground nutmeg

1 **Tbsp** lemon juice

continued

DIRECTIONS (FOR THE FILLING)

Combine all ingredients together, tossing until all the apples are covered.

DIRECTIONS

1. Roll out the bottom crust to fit a **9-inch** pie dish using a rolling pin—try not to handle the dough too much (seeing bits of butter is a good thing—this means a flaky crust!).

2. Spray the bottom of it with non-stick cooking spray or spread the bottom with butter, and place the pie crust in the dish, cutting off the edges to fit.

3. Bake at **350°F** for **4 minutes**, just until the crust bubbles (this is so the bottom won't be soggy).

4. Add filling, and place the other half of the crust on top of the filling.

5. Gather up the edges and pinch the sides. To ventilate, cut three slits on the top of the crust, and place three mostaccioli noodles heads up to let the steam escape.

6. Brush the whole pie with butter and sprinkle with sugar.

7. Bake at **350°F** for **20 minutes** and until the crust is golden brown.

8. Serve HOT with vanilla ice cream or whipped cream (or, if you want to be like Papa, a nice dollop of Cool-Whip).

GREENS: THE GOSTON'S FAMILY RECIPE

BY Asja Goston

As I sneak into the kitchen, I feel a sudden stinging sensation at the back of my neck. My mom has pinched me for dipping into "her" precious pot of greens, insisting the flavors would not be to their full potential if I keep lifting the lid. We both know this is a never-ending story to keep me away.

The aroma of the seasoned mixture of greens is always a familiar scent during special family gatherings. The sacred green vegetable that my family stampedes to the table when receiving is masked with the smell of smoked ham with acidic undertones. Their scents make our bellies groan as if they were striking up a conversation. I am the only brave soul that has enough guts to go into the room where the food is prepared. For me, this is my chance to spruce up the batch to my liking. Extra apple cider vinegar and chicken broth are added if we have any in the cabinet. To learn that these ingredients are key in making the best batch of greens, I have experimented with my own portion at previous gatherings. So, I am certain the chicken broth and extra apple cider vinegar enhance the flavor of the greens, creating a spark that dances on my tongue. I tiptoe into the kitchen to steal a taste of the dish that is "nowhere near ready," as claimed by my mom and grandma, the ones who take care of the dirty work in the kitchen. While my loved ones' backs are turned, I swiftly toss in my secret "kick" to the recipe. I figure if it tastes fantastic no one will notice the difference.

"Collard Greens," more frequently referred to as just "greens," is a dish that consists of, but is not limited to, three bunches of greens, a piece of smoked pork meat, onion, apple cider vinegar, season salt, lemon pepper, and garlic powder. Our family's greens are home-grown. In making collard greens with my mom and grandma, I am assigned to gather spices and clean and cut the greens. Whisking about the kitchen, I search for the spices that are in the cupboard just above the stove. To peek into the cabinet, it is necessary for me to lean forward as much as I can on the balls of my feet. Once my eyes are high enough to see what I am pulling down, the maze-like cabinet becomes simple to conquer. Counting in my head, "1, 2, and 3," I see the spices are all present.

Noticing that the leafy green vegetables need to be stripped from the stems, I walk out the back door leading to the yard. I see the rectangular patch of veggies filled with peppers, tomatoes, and cucumbers, and then I spot the greens. Heading to the right-hand corner closest to the fence, I hurriedly pick the fullest, most vibrant leaves, plucking them from the end of the stem. The leaves are very crunchy and have little bits of dirt on them from the garden. Ripping the stem from the edible parts makes a crisp snap, signaling to me that it's fresh. As I speed through this step of preparation, my mother supervises the way each leaf is divided, hovering over my shoulders. She grumbles at me, "Do not separate the pieces too small; otherwise it will turn out slimy." Continuing to pick the leaves, I watch the way I separate the leaf from the stem—only in halves to insure there aren't any mistakes on my end.

Washing the greens well is vital. When I was growing up, the women in my family taught me to wash the greens in cold water so that they would not wither before the cooking process. Standing in front of the sink is my grammy, filling the kitchen sink with chilled water. She was always, in secret, slickly assisting me without my mom's knowledge. Meeting me at the kitchen sink, with a pile of dirty greens in my hands, Grammy glances at me with a face of sneaky mischief. I give her a sly look back to let her know that I am pleased with her interferences. I dunk the greens into the cold water and start to toss them around. The vicious mixing only lasts thirty seconds. Pulling the vegetables out, I witness grit and dirt lying at the bottom of the sink and floating in the water as it swirls down the drain. While rinsing out the sink, I prepare to repeat the cleaning method twice more to insure cleanliness. When I am done with these tasks, my mom dismisses me from the kitchen area to the living room, where my dad, grandpa, and brothers mingle.

As I step into the room, I am bothered with loudness from the guys trying to talk over one another about sports and video games, or holding heated debates on which movie is better to watch before dinner. I can hear my little brothers beg, "Fortnite is the best free-for-all game. Can we play just a bit longer?" I see my dad get up, with an annoyed look plastered on his face, and turn off the game in the middle of a battle. "It's family time, and no one around you wants to just watch you two play the video game. Spend time with your family," he says. They then flip the station, and before anyone can get an opinioned word out as to what is going to be watched, the channel is briskly changed to ESPN: something all the males agree on.

I think to myself, "These are all things that I do not want to be a part of." I want to be in the kitchen having head-to-head womanly gossip sessions with the mature females in my family.

The Goston family is woven together with all sorts of different racial and cultural backgrounds, such as African American, Sicilian, and some Irish. This dish is inherited from my dad's side of the family, stemming from the southern state of Mississippi. Collard Greens was known as a poor man's dish where my father's family grew up because it was a vegetable that could easily be grown in a garden. Not only that, but the plant's produce would replenish itself at a quick rate. These factors made it a worthy commodity to put time into, as well as gain access of.

"COME TO THE TABLE, IT IS TIME TO EAT!" shouts my mom. The floor vibrates with excitement from everyone's movement rushing into the dining room. I grab my plate, filling it mostly with greens, and walk over to the fridge to add a couple dashes of hot sauce, giving my portion some heat. The sound of lip-smacking as I sit down brings me to the realization that my whole family has gone silent from the satisfying flavors of the sacred greens, which I am silently proud of. The house has finally been filled with the cooling presence of family togetherness.

This meal has always meant a lot to me because it sparks a sense of connectedness within my family that is often hard to find. Being able to catch the laughter of the gossipy women in the kitchen, who put a trace of themselves in every dish, as well as observing the obnoxious men getting rowdy with my younger brothers, gives me a sense of peace, knowing my family is whole.

. . .

COLLARD GREENS

INGREDIENTS

3 bunches of greens

Smoked ham hocks or smoked turkey neckbones

Onion

Apple cider vinegar

Season salt

Lemon pepper

Garlic powder (measured by taste)

DIRECTIONS

1. Pick the greens, and wash them well in cold water.
2. Cut up the onion into small pieces.
3. Throw all ingredients in a large pot, except for the meat, and boil with seasonings/vinegar.
4. Boil the smoked meat in a separate pot for about **1 hour**, then combine the little pot with the larger pot.
5. Keep boiling, while tasting to see if more seasoning or vinegar is needed.
6. Boil until tender.

ASJA'S SECRET INGREDIENTS

Chicken broth and extra apple cider vinegar.

THE DEWEERD SHRIMP BOIL: UNITING A FAMILY ONE TOTE AT A TIME

BY Caleb DeWeerd

CLANG! My Uncle Todd and my dad next to me burst into whoops of celebration and mockery as the neck-and-neck game ends. I look down again as if maybe I only imagined it, but the two rusting arms of the horseshoe embrace the stake for a perfect "ringer." Walking across the spotted grass that spans the two pits, my grandpa and I console each other, as has happened many times over the years. Horseshoes is one of the games the DeWeerd men consider a tradition during the annual DeWeerd camping trip, and I rarely walk away the victor. Despite the brief sting of a loss or rush of winning, however, it is simply a joy to be able to play among the grown men of the family. Growing up, and still to this day, playing with the dads produces a feeling of manhood, almost like a rite of passage. Horseshoes is especially significant on Saturday afternoon because it always precedes the shrimp boil. After a few games between grandsons, fathers, and Grandpa, the unspoken cue is given and we walk back to camp to begin preparations.

For the grandkids, the first thing to be done is to peel the ears of corn. Groans can be heard as tired bodies are pulled from their different activities but the complaints soon become laughing and joking. As the plump, yellow ears of corn begin to emerge from the husks, Grandma directs the hunt for and preparation of the other ingredients. The aunts and uncles diligently set to work thawing the shrimp, peeling and quartering the potatoes, and slicing the sausage. As the camp settles into an organized chaos, Grandpa brings out the twenty-year-old aluminum pot for yet another annual shrimp boil. When one aunt marvels to him how clean and new it looks year after year, he simply replies, "Bar Keepers Friend and a little hard scrubbing, baby." When Grandpa has it filled and the water is at a rolling boil, it is time for the ingredients. The chunks of potato are the first in because of the extra time they require, but after five minutes by themselves, the sausage, shrimp, and halved sweet corn join them. Because of the high temperature, the boil itself takes only ten to fifteen minutes. But when Grandma is the director, there is no time for idle hands.

When the grocery bags of husks, corn silk, and empty meat packaging have been brought to the dumpster, it is all hands on deck to arrange picnic tables, chairs, and side dishes. Being the two eldest grandsons, my cousin Alex and I have the job of moving the picnic tables under the screen tents. This leaves the middle grandkids to get the camp chairs set in a circle around the fire pit, and the older granddaughters to help the aunts get all the side dishes set onto the serving table. At this point in the process, the sights and smells that fill the campsite are beginning to arouse the rumbling giants of hungry stomachs. As the complementary dishes begin to emerge from their coolers, mouths begin to water. Aunt Paulette's famous tapioca fruit salad, Aunt Kris's pesto pasta and berry spinach salads, Aunt Erin's heaping bowl of bright red watermelon, Grandma's potato salad and her renowned onion sauce for the shrimp boil, and my mom's Orzo pasta and snicker salads all adorn the old, blue checkered tablecloth that somehow lasts from year to year. The remaining space between the established dishes is occupied by newcomers. These are the dishes experimented on throughout the year and deemed delicious enough to make their debut on this special weekend. The end of the food table is the place of honor, however, because this is where the main dish resides. For more than twenty years, it has been the staple of every DeWeerd summer camping trip. Rain or shine, new campground or frequented one, the shrimp boil has its mark on each and every one. Because of its consistency, it is now a symbol of our family and the traditions we hold dear. Not only that, it also brings to mind all the emotions and memories that make our family what it is. From difficulties that we have shared like cancer in the family to joys like the addition of a new member to the DeWeerd clan, our experiences are what makes up our foundation. My grandpa placing the Rubbermaid tote piled to overflowing with steaming vegetables and meat is the signal for the family to gather round. With stomachs rumbling like distant thunder and mouths watering in anticipation, we quiet our hearts and slow our minds from the frenzied pace of preparing the food as Grandpa leads us in prayer. This prayer is one of praise as we thank God for his great faithfulness and the blessings he has given us.

While the food and flavors are delicious, the people are what makes this tradition special. Every year, I find myself looking around the circle of people that I call family and being filled with joy to the point of overflowing. In part, it is knowing that I am loved. I know that no matter how much time goes by, how far apart we grow, or what mistakes I make, that I am loved and accepted by these people. This lesson is something Grandpa has stressed to us grandkids for as long as I can remember: We can keep on fighting the good fight in whatever strength God has given us because we know we are already accepted. We do not need to earn acceptance, nor could we ever hope to. God has purchased us at a price and we are his children and therefore, we can live boldly as leaders in this world. My grandpa and grandma's lives are a testimony to the Lord's faithfulness towards those who love him and seek him and are willing to be guided by his will.

This shrimp boil is far more than just a symphony of flavorful food. It is a symbol of who the DeWeerd family is. It represents the love we have for each other, it represents the bond we share, and most importantly, it stands as a monument in my memory to the steadfast faithfulness of the Lord. It is a reminder that the Lord is good and his love endures forever.

• • •

SHRIMP BOIL

INGREDIENTS

5 lbs potatoes, quartered

3 lbs sausage

3 lbs shrimp (tails on or off)

Sweet corn, halved

DIRECTIONS

Bring water to boil in large pot. Add potatoes and allow to boil for **5 minutes**. Then add sausage, corn, and shrimp. Allow to cook for **10** to **15 minutes** or until potatoes are to your preferred tenderness. Drain away water and then dump into a large container when ready. Allow **5** to **10 minutes** to cool.

JANCHI GUKSU: THE NOODLE DISH

BY Shinhye Hwang

The heat is unbearable, I thought to myself as I did my homework. The hot weather of Cambodia had not decided to be gracious this day. Sweat ran down my back and soaked my buttoned-up blue school uniform. Even from the fourth floor of my apartment, I could hear the voices of children playing outside. The sun slowly started to set, mixing red and orange throughout the sky. I was tired, sleepy, and hungry from having to go through another day of school. I was on the verge of drifting off to sleep when I caught a particular smell. There were no words to describe it, other than that it was delicious. This is the way with most Korean foods; it's hard to place an adjective to the smell of a Korean dish. Still, the scent that I smelled—I would recognize it anywhere.

I immediately got up from my seat, left my room, and passed the shelves of books filling up the hallway. My sister came out from the room as well, smelling the same smell I did. Both of us had neglected to ask my mom what we were having for dinner that day. Usually, we would ask her that question the moment we got comfortable in the car, heading home from school. It was one of the few things my sister and I had in common: we were always wondering what's for dinner.

As I headed towards the aroma, I heard the sound of a knife hitting the cutting board with a steady, constant rhythm. In the kitchen was my mom, chopping carrots into long, thin pieces.

"What are we having today?" I asked enthusiastically.

"*Janchi Guksu*," she replied. My sister scrunched her face, said "Ugh," and went back to the room. I cheered and stayed a bit longer, lurking in the kitchen, taking in the aromatic smell of the dish not yet completed.

Janchi Guksu, otherwise known as "Korean Warm Noodle Soup," is a food that includes somyeon noodles (white, round noodles), anchovy broth, vegetables (carrots, cucumbers, squash), minced beef, and eggs. The noodles need to be boiled in water until cooked, then drained and left on the side. The minced beef and vegetables will then be cooked on a pan with a small drizzle of oil. The eggs need to be stirred together first so that the whites and the yolks mix, and then cooked in the pan. After that, the egg and the vegetables need to be chopped into thin pieces about 0.25cm wide and 5cm long (1/10 of an inch by 2 inches). Next, add the noodles to the warm anchovy broth, which should be poured in separate bowls for each person. Each of them could add as much of the vegetables and eggs as they liked. The cook can also make a sauce called *Yangnyeomjang*, which consists of soy sauce, chili pepper flakes, sesame oil, sesame seeds, chopped scallions, and garlic. The sauce should be set aside so that those who want to put it in their broth can add as much or as little as they wish.

In Korean history, this food was usually eaten during special events such as weddings and birthday parties. In a way it can be seen as a Korean casserole. In those days, when people wore *Hanbok* (a traditional, beautiful two-piece clothing which was made of silk with elegant patterns as embroidery), flour was very rare. The milling technology used to make noodles was from the Western nations, and without the technology it was hard to make long noodles. Koreans, who were used to eating hard wheats like millet, thought that eating soft noodles was good for the body. They even went so far as to believe that the food *Janchi Guksu* would let them live a longer life.

Now the food has become common in restaurants, yet not too common in households. But here I was, in my blue uniform and khaki pants, in my house, in a foreign country, with nothing special to celebrate. My mom had purchased the long, white noodles, dried anchovies, eggs, and the minced meat from a nearby Korean mart that was a short ten minutes away from the house. The fresh vegetables were purchased at a Cambodian market about twenty minutes away by car. Soy sauce, sesame oil, salt, pepper, and sugar were always available in the house since they were the basic ingredients for any good Korean dish and must-have ingredients for any Korean household. My parents will often offer us a famous side dish of spicy and sweet cabbage, known as *kimchi*, but I always politely decline. My parents don't understand why. Most Koreans eat it with just about anything. Some might even say they can't live without it.

Then again, I am not like most Koreans. I was born in Korea, yet have lived in Cambodia for fourteen years. Not only have I been in a different country, but I have been going to an international school since kindergarten, one that teaches in English. So I have a mix of Korean, Cambodian, and American culture in me. I am definitely not your typical Korean.

I asked my mom if I could help her with anything.

Even though we are in the modern era and ingredients are easier to get, the time it takes to make the food hasn't changed. There were still more vegetables to be chopped and fried. Yet, just like every other time I've asked, she shook her head and told me to go back and do my homework. I groaned inwardly and dragged myself back to my room, bringing my grumbling stomach along with me.

Dinner time soon came, though, and my family sat around the table. My mom had already poured the anchovy broth into each of our bowls. The chopped vegetables, meat, and eggs were all on a plate in neat, sorted piles. The cooked noodles were also in neat, round piles; they looked like spaghetti noodles twirled into a pile. My family prayed together, then started to dig into the food.

My sister did what I expected her to. She put in only the eggs and minced meat. My mom told her to put in some vegetables, but she didn't listen. She was in her sophomore year of high school, yet was still picky about her food. My dad put everything in: vegetables, minced meat, eggs, the sauce, even the *kimchi*. I couldn't wait to try the food as everyone else measured out their chosen toppings. I wanted to feel the savory taste of broth and noodles spread throughout my tongue as I chewed and swallowed. Here I was, part of a Korean household living in Cambodia, enjoying a special holiday meal on a school day.

• • •

JANCHI GUKSU

INGREDIENTS & DIRECTIONS

1. BROTH

Add green onions, **3 pieces** of kelp, and **15-20** anchovies into the water and boil; once the broth starts boiling, take out the pieces of kelp and add in the green onions.

Boil then let it cool.

2. SAUCE

Add some soy sauce to the water to the point where it's not yet salty.

Dice the chives and add diced garlic with chili powder, sesame seeds, and sesame oil to the soy sauce and water.

3. GARNISH*

Cut carrots, onions, and squash into long, thin pieces; then fry in small amount of oil.

Mix the egg yolk and egg white together, then fry in the pan—once finished, cut the fried egg into long, thin pieces.

Add some soy sauce, a bit of garlic, sugar, and pepper— pour drizzle of oil into the frying pan, then cook the minced beef.

Cut the cucumbers into long, thin strips—do not fry; leave it raw.

Cut *kimchi* into small bits (optional).

continued

4. NOODLES

Boil the water.

Put noodles into boiling water—one serving is about the size of a quarter.

Once the water starts to boil, add some water to lessen the temperature—repeat about three times (this process makes the noodles more chewy).

When you think the noodles are cooked through, take out the noodles and place them in cold water—use both hands to rub the noodles against each other—repeat process twice—wash once more in cold water.

Place cooked noodles on wicker tray to get rid of water.

Put noodles in the bowl first then add garnish (carrots, onions, squash, eggs, cucumber, beef, and *kimchi*)—add broth.

* Add garnish according to your appetite.

KEATING POTATOES: A FOOD TO CONNECT US

BY Hannah Keating

My dad pulls into the driveway of my mom's house to pick us all up. My three younger siblings and I jump in, rushing off to the grocery store. We are always in charge of last-minute groceries for dinner. Once we arrive there, I am the one, being the oldest, who runs in, retrieving anything needed to complete our Thanksgiving dinner.

I am almost done picking up all the necessary foods when I pass the vegetable section. The colorful array is similar to the one I will see on the table at my aunt's house, considering we make almost every possible food you could imagine for Thanksgiving. Coming from a large family, we need large amounts and many varieties of food to fill everyone's belly on this special occasion.

Rushing out of the store and to the family party, I feel my stomach start to yearn for our special family dish. I walk up my aunt's porch, on the same day I do every year, holding three bags of groceries. My family swarms around my siblings and me. Although we never go more than a few weeks without a family gathering, they greet us as if they have not seen us in years. This particular time is special though; Thanksgiving is a celebration held with honor in the Keating household.

Even though my grandparents were both 100% Irish,

they never lived in Ireland. They met in college while attending Notre Dame and eventually had a big family. My dad grew up with seven siblings, Pam, Paul, Diane, Mark, Kathy, Suzie, Karen, and Mike. While raising their children, my grandparents held up Irish Catholic traditions. On holidays, Irish food was always hauled out. Copious amounts of corned beef and cabbage lined the tables and countertops.

Ireland is known for having dishes with potatoes in them so we always had them, too. All of my dad's siblings were picky eaters, so on holidays my grandma made something for everyone so they could enjoy the meal. Everyone agreed on one dish, a specialty of the family: Keating potatoes. It was my grandma's own recipe, which we still use today.

Grandma always started with six of the best red potatoes she could find, and then grated them slowly. The smell of melting butter would trigger the sweet aromas of the recipe's ingredients. She would grate two cups of cheddar cheese before adding in the good stuff, one whole carton of sour cream. After tossing everything in, she added green onions, salt, and pepper and mixed it all together. My grandma baked the potatoes in the oven for 45 minutes, filling the air with the warm smell of our family's dish. Excitement would fill the hearts of my father and his siblings as the aromas swept the room. Soon, the food producing that smell would fill their bellies. Family members would remind one another that Keating potatoes should not be consumed often. No arteries in the world could handle such a food regularly. Now, despite my never having met my grandmother, I still enjoy the tradition she passed down to her daughters. It's her dish that brings us all together.

Back at the Keating household, I am on work crew. Since it is Thanksgiving, I am in a good mood and do not mind putting in a little extra work. I start stirring, setting up, and baking whatever my aunts tell me to while they do the real cooking. Only they prepare the potatoes on special holidays for the whole family. Today, we make double batches. We rotate as to who takes the extras home, but there are never any Keating potatoes to spare. After asking my aunts, I now know my grandmother's secret recipe. The little ones still do not know what makes them special, but one day they will.

We gather around the kitchen island to say grace together. God blesses me immensely. I am grateful to spend time with my family and share such a delicious meal this year. As the prayer wraps up, I chime in, remembering the last line: "Father, Son, and Holy Ghost, whoever eats the fastest gets the most!" My grandpa passed down this saying, and we recite it now right before the family of 50+ swarms the food table. Grabbing double scoops of Keating potatoes and sides of turkey, my cousins and I run to our favorite seats in the house.

Sitting around the former kid's table, we enjoy a bite of our family's dish. The smell of green onions launches off our plates and dances up to warm our lungs. I finish all of my food in under 15 minutes flat, a new record. Nothing brings my family closer together than enjoying our favorite dish. Food brightens the mood. Everyone smiles and laughs on Thanksgiving. Adults drink a little too much, leading the kids who are old enough to take their place as designated drivers.

Before walking out of my aunt's house, I make a round trip to each floor, saying goodbye to every family member. I never leave anyone out. With leftovers warming my hands, I close the door, ending another successful holiday. Food bonds us like no other, and the Keating potatoes keep tradition close to our hearts.

. . .

KEATING POTATOES

INGREDIENTS & DIRECTIONS

1. 6 medium red potatoes—grate on largest cut.

2. Slowly melt ¼ cup butter and 2 cups shredded cheese.

3. Add 2 cups sour cream, ⅓ cup chopped green onion, 1 tsp salt and ½ tsp pepper.

4. Toss with grated potatoes. Place in greased warm baking dish. Bake 45 minutes at 350°F.

MOLE POBLANO: MY FOOD STORY

BY **Paulette Atenco**

My eyes slowly open but then quickly reclose. The sunlight shining through my blinds is overwhelming. Somehow I force myself to turn over and reach for the phone on my nightstand. It's 2:43 p.m. Having to get up early this morning for church has prompted this afternoon nap, a Sunday ritual. My final moments burrowed in the sheets end abruptly with my mother's call. That gets me out of bed and on my feet real quick. The longer I take to respond, the greater the chance that my mom gets mad at me. I start to run down the stairs but stop midway when I hear the electric blender going. Then I hear water running into the sink, then the chime of our oven, the sign that a preheated temperature has been met. But the most important thing to hit me is that smell. It is so potent and thick, much like the consistency of the sauce. I can already taste the mixture of chocolate and spice. All of this tells me two things: we are expecting company, and we are serving them the usual, enchiladas with *mole*.

I cautiously finish going down the stairs because I can never tell whether having people come over will lead to harmony or a complete warzone. My mom is a total extrovert. She loves people and parties. Any social event there is, my mother volunteers to host. She would have people over every day if not for my dad. Sandalio is mostly anti-social. My parents' marriage is the poster child for the "Opposites Attract" philosophy. They could not be more different from one another. That being said, having guests over often results in conflict, which then leads to division and bickering, not something I want to be caught in the middle of.

As I walk into the kitchen, everything seems to be okay. My mom is overlooking the stove. Sandalio is washing some dishes. Samantha, my 28-year-old sister, is cutting vegetables. All of this is happening to the soundtrack of cumbias and norteños, which can best be described as mariachi music. I cautiously ease into the kitchen, knowing that in a matter of seconds I will be appointed a job. "Poetita, haz me un favor. Debone this chicken," my mother tells me. I always get this job when we make enchiladas with *mole*. I absolutely *hate* this job. Having to debone and shred boiled chicken always leaves me smelling like poultry for the rest of the day.

I'm sure there are many Hispanic young adults who have gotten stuck with this job and feel my pain because *mole* isn't just an Atenco recipe. *Mole poblano*, its proper name, is actually the most popular dish from our region, Puebla, Mexico. The origin of *mole poblano* is a much debated topic. Some claim that Italians were the first to invent *mole* and that it was later brought to and adapted by the Poblanos, residents of Puebla. Others disagree, saying that *mole's* origins derive from the Aztecs because the word *mole* is similar to the Aztec word for a sauce or concoction, *moll*. Still others say that *mole* was simply a happy accident from chocolate falling into stew. I personally side with the argument for an Aztec origin, due to pride in my heritage. Sandalio would kill me otherwise.

Although deboning chicken comes at a smelly cost, my mom has been dealt the hardest hand. *Mole* is no walk in the park. Traditionally, it cooks for hours and hours, not to mention the actual process of creating the *mole*. The most labor-intensive part of the process is grinding the spices in the *metate*. A *metate* is a stone tool used for grinding down whole spices, nuts, seeds, and chilies. There are two parts to a *metate*: the stone "bowl" and the pestle, a blunt club-shaped object. My mother combines the chilies, sesame seeds, raisins, and garlic cloves in the *metate*, takes the pestle in her hand, and lets the rhythmic arm movements and strength take care of the rest. I've watched her do this ever since I could look over the counter. She's let me try the *metate* a couple of times, but within thirty seconds I'm begging her to take over. It takes a lot out of your arm, but it's a vital step to getting that spicy but sweet flavor my family and I have grown so fond of over the years.

To our dismay, our guests, my mother's side of the family, have only given us two hours to prepare for their visit. As much as there is to do within those two hours, I cannot wait for them to pass. My mother's side of the family is pretty wonderful—but it's my grandparents that bring joy to my soul. Grandpa Jacinto is so comical and silly. He always has scruff on his chin, which he purposely grows out just so he can trick me. It's the same routine with him. He'll reach out to hold my hand, stroke it for a bit, and then, when I'm least expecting it, rub it against his coarse stubble. It feels like sandpaper. I've caught onto his trick by now, of course, but I still play along to get a laugh out of him. Grandpa Jacinto also never shies away from speaking his mind. Whether that is a positive characteristic or not is still up for discussion, especially among restaurant managers and waitresses, who might question my grandpa's "freedom of speech."

Thank God for my grandpa's keeper, my Grandma Roma. I know people always claim their grandma is the best, but I challenge all of those allegations. I know my grandma is sweeter still and more precious. Just thinking of her makes me feel warm and secure. She has the softest skin known to humankind and always smells like Downy fabric softener. Although she is kindhearted and nurturing, you wouldn't want to get on her bad side. Just like the rest of the women in our family, Grandma Roma can be as sassy and smart-mouthed as she can be sweet. Maybe all of the spice in our culture's cuisine has leaked into our blood stream, causing us to be a pretty feisty family.

Just as I set down the last table setting, the doorbell rings. Our guests, my family, have arrived. Now the smells of *mole* and chicken will be accompanied by the sounds of laughter and love. A lot of things can bring people together, but I have found food to be the most effective. As I cut into my *mole*-covered enchilada and indulge in that first forkful, the flavor is out of this world. I look around and see eyes rolling and hear "Mmm!" escaping everyone's mouth. All of that work and preparation has once again paid off.

I can't help but think of the past and future generations of my people who have experienced or will experience this culinary sensation. I just hope they experience the same love and closeness my family and I do when we sit down to eat *mole poblano*. It's one thing to eat a good, well-prepared meal; but to eat a good, well-prepared meal in good company is completely different. Let me tell you a little secret. The second option is the better and more satisfying of the two.

• • •

MOLE

INGREDIENTS

1 whole chicken, cooked and shredded

1 lb chile pasilla, roasted and cut into small pieces

½ cup raisins

1 ripe plantain, fried and sliced

¼ cup sesame seeds, roasted

5 cloves garlic, roasted

1 tortilla

1 onion, grilled/roasted

1 oz Abuelita chocolate, broken into pieces

3 Tbsps vegetable oil

1 cup chicken broth

DIRECTIONS

1. Combine the chiles, onion, garlic, sesame seeds, tortilla, raisins, and cloves. Puree small amounts of this mixture in a blender until smooth.

2. Fry the mixture in a little oil and add the chicken stock slowly, stirring frequently, over a very low heat for **45 minutes**. The sauce should be thick.

3. When it's ready, ladle *mole* sauce over cooked chicken pieces.

LET'S CALL IT CASSEROLE

BY **Raeann Fopma**

It always starts with a burnt mouth. My haste to dig into the food on my cracked plastic tray leads to a steaming mouth and scorched tongue. The fire in my mouth doesn't deter me for long, however, for there is more green bean casserole to be eaten.

In my family, Thanksgiving holds court around a nicked ping pong table in the heart of a Dutch community called Pella. The basement of my grandma's house holds dish upon dish of every sort of potato, turkey, vegetable, and dessert. They line the table, steam wafting into the air as each course is uncovered. Smells of cheesy potatoes and gravy fill the room, and the many mouths that crowd the basement begin to water. After trudging through the line to get my food, I find my spot at one of the many folding tables set up for the occasion, my chair creaking beneath me as I settle in.

Where to begin? Most would start with the turkey, which always seems to be the center of attention on this particular day, or perhaps the cheesy potatoes. An indulgent few might even begin with a bite of pumpkin pie or some chocolatey confection. Me? My fork zeroes in on the seemingly unassuming green bean casserole. Loading the first bite with a hefty serving of the beans, with extra fried onions mixed in of course, I endure a burnt mouth—year after year.

My family is one hundred percent Dutch. Both my mom's and my dad's family originated in the Netherlands, from the province of Friesland. So we have a strong Dutch heritage. My grandma still prides herself in sewing Dutch costumes for all of us, so that we can scrub the streets of Pella in authentic dress during the town's annual Tulip Time—a three-day celebration of all things Dutch. Although we strongly identify as Dutchmen, other than the occasional *stroopwafel* or *poffertje*, our ancestry is not very present in the foods we eat. Instead, our meals are Midwestern through and through. Green bean casserole is a great example of that: it's simple, cost-effective, and not the least bit ostentatious. It's in this way that the food my family puts on our table reflects who we are, and how we live.

When my ancestors migrated to the United States from the Netherlands, they had to learn to make do with only a little. Settling in south-central Iowa, with hopes of making a living off of the abundant farmland, the Dutchmen adopted a very frugal lifestyle. Phrases like, "Don't throw that food away, it'll make good leftovers" or "If you take it, you better eat it" are thrown around during holidays with my family, and a case of spilled milk becomes a tragedy. We might also be fed all the leftovers that could be found in the fridge, mixed in a crockpot, and called *casserole*.

In the wallpaper-clad, brown carpeted basement, bent and fading playing cards are scattered across the folding table, chairs creak, and stories fill the air. I grew up hearing tales of my dad's escapades on the family farm, of all the trouble he and his brothers and sisters got into. Their stories wrap around me like a patchwork quilt of Shetland ponies, sleds going down ice-covered hills, gravel-road journeys on a yellow school bus, and muggy Iowa Augusts spent playing slow pitch softball. Some stories are repeated more often than others, like "the time the gun went off in the basement" or the unforgettable "tractor-tipping incident." With the tales of adventure and danger come others of long hours spent barn-painting and pig-tending and fence-repairing. Conversation echoes through the basement as young cousins zoom toy cars by. Adults lay claim to overstuffed chairs that have been around longer than I have. The tastes they now treasure run parallel to the stories of my Dutch-transplant, thoroughly Iowan family.

My family's cuisine has never been an extravagant one. We enjoy mild flavors, big portions, and an abundance of casseroles. I don't think there's a way of cooking potatoes that we haven't yet discovered. These familiar flavors suit my tall, mild-mannered, hardworking relatives. We Dutchmen are a people that flourished here in the Midwest because of our initiative, and because of our lack of indulgence. Our avoidance of all things non-essential aided us in surviving the immigration to America, but don't think for a minute that we lack any sort of flavor.

• • •

GREEN BEAN CASSEROLE

INGREDIENTS

Milk

Salt and pepper

2 cups sliced green beans

1 (**10.75-oz**) **can** cream of mushroom soup

1 (**2.8-oz**) **can** French-fried onion rings

½ **cup** cheddar cheese

DIRECTIONS

Preheat the oven to **350°F.** Add the mushroom soup and milk (fill the soup can with milk to measure) to the green beans. Add salt and pepper and onions. Stir well. Pour into a greased **1.5-quart** baking dish. Bake for **20 minutes,** then top the casserole with the cheddar and more French-fried onions and bake for **10 minutes** longer, or until the casserole is hot and cheese is melted.

. . .

Green bean casserole is an unquestionable staple in my home. Every Christmas, every Thanksgiving, every Easter, or any other special occasion is sure to have at least one dish of it. Green bean casserole originated in 1955 when the Campbell's soup company created the recipe by adding their cream of mushroom soup to frozen green beans. The Midwest's love for quick and easy recipes, as well as casseroles of any sort, made the meal an instant hit. The quick and easy dish has been in my family for as long as I can remember. Ever since I was old enough to recall those cramped Thanksgiving afternoons, green bean casserole has been on the table.

GEMÜTLICHKEIT

BY Alexandria Eggert

My knees knock against the bottom of the red pleather card table as my sister and cousin rush to their seats. I know I'm too tall to sit here comfortably but I can't resist the nostalgia of the plush table top under my plate-laden hands. Here we sat for our beloved *butterbrot* snack, our "Intro to *Froebel* Star Folding" lessons, and stories from Oma all the while. Stories of hardship in the war-ravaged Germany she came from, of family she looked after while her parents worked tirelessly, of love that tore her from the life she knew in Germany to follow the US soldier, our Opa, to the US. I was never sure where I belonged in those stories, or where those stories belonged as a part of me. In many ways, my curiosity regarding my heritage began at that table above dishes like this one.

As I set down my plate, the deep, rich aromas of vinegar, bay, brown sugar, and apple float from the heap of sauerkraut and dance under my nose. I knew the rib-capped mountain of pickled cabbage would remain unfinished. Despite half-hearted protests of "No, that's enough, I won't be able to finish it all," Oma continued scooping while chuckling "*Achk*, Ally you need to eat more." But more isn't needed with this food. Germans are descendants of hearty clans, clans that survived harsh winters and fought off Roman armies. No matter how fragile my family may think I am, I always took pride in that. The food that Germans eat is just as effective as it is succulent, reasonable looking portions puffing the stomach as though you had eaten three of the American meals once foreign to my mother. Although there would be waste, I cherished the sight of one of the succulent ribs melting off the bone and sinking into the pile of golden sauerkraut below.

During our family's annual trip to Milwaukee's Germanfest, my eyes would drown in the swirling rainbow pools of plaid *dirndls* speckled with heavy earth-toned *lederhosen* amidst the crowds of t-shirt and short-clad attendees. Red paint would be chipped off the weathered long tables where rows of plates were gathered from the surrounding stands of potato pancake, pickled herring, Usinger sausage, and *spanferkel*. A brassy *"Ein prosit! Ein prosit! Der Gemütlichkeit!"* is bellowed out from the now standing and swaying crowd. Frosted mugs and the occasional ornate stein are tipped back for a drink. When the ritual is finished, I ask Oma what it means. She cannot say at first. There are many more words in German that do not translate to English as well as I would like. "Like *together*," she says "like we are family, we all are together and happy like a family. We belong together." By the end of the night the song has been sung one too many times, and as the swirling pools still to stammering, torpid, beer-drunk puddles, my parents politely usher our family to the exit gates. My mind begins to wander. Did Oma grow up wearing the same dresses? Did she fold the same stars? Dance and sing the same ways? Eat the same food? Could this day have been my daily experience if Opa had decided to stay with her in Germany?

Every bite of sauerkraut, every bit of story, every note

of accordion, stomp of foot, swish of plaid, slosh of beer brought to me this one question: What was Germany really like? Not the foreign, barbaric, harsh, evil Germany you see in textbooks, but the Germany that Oma missed so much that she painted verbal pictures of it every moment my cousin, sister, or I asked. Stories are a deep tradition in Germany. They were for us, too. At dinner, over plates of sauerkraut and pork, Oma would read in her native tongue the same tales German children had heard for centuries. Hansel and Gretel creak open the German witch's cottage door, Cinderella dances in the ballroom of a German castle, and Little Red Riding Hood skips through the German forest in my head. These stories taught me my German and my Germany, a gothic wood painting of a tall white castle rising from a dark, tangled forest.

I would discover the answers to all these mysteries myself, in Oma's home country. As I lifted the latch of the white fence gate, my stomach felt as full of butterflies as did Hansel's, Gretel's, Cinderella's, and Little Red Riding Hood's when they opened their doors to the unknown. In front of my sister and me stood a stout, unfamiliar man as we shook out the words we were taught to say, "*Bist du mein Onkel Wilfred?*" A burst of screams, laughter, and hugs came from all around as estranged aunts, great aunts, uncles, great uncles, cousins, and second cousins flowed from the car behind us and the square house in front of us. This was home. This was belonging. This was *Gemütlichkeit*.

During our family vacation to Europe in 2008, we were able to reunite with Oma's family in Nürnberg, Germany. Germany was not the austere, cold mystery I had been taught, but something I unwittingly knew. I saw the cottage-like house where Oma grew up with her numerous siblings; I saw boats lowered into the Danube canal; I saw the open fields blur past the car windows and thought of Oma bringing supplies home to her family, picking potato bugs from the plants scattered there during WWII. Panning through a vast array of ornate *dirndls* to find my purple and green dress trimmed with ornately woven ribbon, I found Oma was not ecstatic at its beauty, as blue and brown, not purple and green, were the colors of her hometown. Without doubt, the food they ate was the same as I had enjoyed in Oma's kitchen. Our first night we sat around a sturdy wooden table in red cushioned seats and dug into forkfuls of sauerkraut, sausage, and rib that exuded vinegar, bay, brown sugar, and apple. "Sauerkraut was always a natural favorite," Oma explained, as the cabbage was homegrown, free, and delicious. Other nights the sauerkraut, sausage, and pork followed us to the aged, wooden *Hofbräuhaus* nearby, where the familiar drunken strains of *"Ein Prosit"* were heard above the chatter of united family. *Das ist Gemütlichkeit.*

Upon returning to the United States, I carried my newfound home in Germany with me. Watching Oma chop up juicy red apples and golden onions, strain sweet sauerkraut, and lay fresh ribs in the pan, we heard new stories sparked by our new memories of Germany. Oma had eaten this dish every Sunday promptly at noon, made with cabbage, onion, potatoes, and tomatoes from her garden to save the little money her family had. Between three and four in the afternoon was coffee hour, when they would eat any number of decadent homemade cakes. The rich taste of Oma's meals brings me back to the stone roads, gothic town houses, and *Gemütlichkeit* of Germany. In keeping with tradition, the plates with rolling hills of sauerkraut met by a rib-bone bridge were removed from the red pleather table and replaced with honeyed, almond-dotted *beinenstich*. As the American notes of coffee cover the German scents of vinegar, bay, brown sugar, and apple, we exchange stories of our journeys in Germany, of family, of *Gemütlichkeit*.

• • •

PORK RIBS WITH SAUERKRAUT

INGREDIENTS

3 (14-oz) cans Frank's Sweet Bavarian Style Kraut

1 cup chopped yellow onion

1 cup brown sugar

1 apple, chopped

3 bay leaves

3 Wyler's beef cubes

3 lbs pork ribs, bone-in

DIRECTIONS

Preheat oven to 350°F. Layer the following mixtures and ingredients in a large casserole dish or roasting pan:

1. Mix the sauerkraut with the onion, brown sugar, and apple and add to pan.

2. Drain the sauerkraut and mix the resulting liquid with the beef cubes and pour into pan.

3. Add bay leaves.

4. Lay ribs on top.

DO NOT STIR. Cover the dish with foil and bake at 350°F for 3 hours. Remove foil and bake for the last 45 minutes.

HIMBASHA: BREAD OF BLESSING

BY Naomi Araya

My sister and I are the first generation in my family to be born in America. Both our parents are immigrants. My mom was born in Ethiopia and my dad in Eritrea. The two countries were once one but split after the war that took place from May 6, 1998, to May 25, 2000. Although the two countries have had their issues since then, many people still consider them one. The culture of both countries is the exact same. The only difference is their language. In Eritrea, the main language spoken is Tigrinya; in Ethiopia, it is Amharic. When I went to Eritrea in 2004 I was starstruck by the culture, and since then I have wanted to hold it tightly.

When I was a young girl, my grandma cooked traditional food every day for my family. We barely ate any other food because we were so immersed in our culture, and food was a big part of culture. To my grandma, this meant preparing food the day we would eat it, not the night before or weeks in advance. She would make *himbasha* for our family, a traditional bread that can be eaten with butter, honey, cream cheese, coffee, tea, or milk, though milk was usually available only on special occasions. I remember watching her make the bread and asking her if I could pattern a small, personal *himbasha* the way she did hers.

She showed me how to use a fork to imprint different lines and patterns into my small loaf.

Himbasha is never made the night before. The dough is prepared a few hours in advance and then is covered so it can rise. Most often it's made plain but it also can be made with raisins or with different grains. My mom will usually make several of the doughs and have each one sit out in pans or bowls until it rises when she bakes it in the oven or on the stove top. Though my mom makes the bread when we request it, *himbasha* is usually made for special occasions. When a child turns one, for example, *himbasha* is placed on the child's back and broken in half. Traditionally, this represents future prosperity and blessings for the baby. It symbolizes good health, safety, and a multitude of blessings.

We had our own *himbasha* celebration last year when my niece, Saige, turned one. The extended family and some close family friends gathered in my brother and sister-in-law's house. The night before, my great-grandma had flown in from Virginia. On the way back from the airport, she and my brother stopped at a grocery store to get the ingredients she would need to bake the *himbasha* the next morning. My brothers-in-law also drove up from Missouri, so we had a full house. My great-grandma slept on a bed in baby Saige's room while I slept on an air mattress on the floor.

The next morning the sun peaked out from behind the clouds and a warm breeze flowed in through the window. My great-grandma, brother, sister-in-law, her parents, her brothers, my parents, and I woke up early, played traditional music, did some dancing, and set out to clean the house. It had such a lively feel inside. The two moms and my sister-in-law set out to prepare the food while the two dads and my brother set tables and chairs outside, set up the speakers, and put the tents up. I bathed my niece and got her ready for the party. I clothed her with the light pink dress with a flower pattern and pink headband that had been laid out on her bed and slipped on her new pair of white sandals. Holding her gently in my arms, I carried her downstairs and played with her outside. In the afternoon, with the party ready to begin, my great-grandma humbly prayed over the food we had prepared for our guests.

Soon after dinner, my mom made an announcement that it was time for the blessing. My sister-in-law held baby Saige, with my brother right beside her. My great-grandma then took the bread and broke it over little Saige's back. Everyone started cheering when baby Saige received the blessing. We gathered for family pictures, and then the music grew louder and people started dancing again. I took the bread and cut it into pieces, distributing it among our guests as we all celebrated the life God had given this child we loved. Something Eritrean and Ethiopian had followed us to America.

• • •

HIMBASHA

INGREDIENTS

1 (7-g) **sachet** dried yeast

55 g (¼ **cup**) caster sugar

600 g (4 **cups**) plain flour

2 **tsps** black sesame seeds

2 **tsps** ground cardamom

80 ml (⅓ **cup**) vegetable oil

Melted butter, to serve

COOK'S NOTES

We use Australian tablespoons and cups: 1 **tsp** equals 5 **ml**; 1 **Tbsp** equals 20 **ml**; 1 **cup** equals 250 **ml**. All herbs are fresh (unless specified), and cups are lightly packed.

DIRECTIONS

1. Dissolve yeast in 250 **ml** lukewarm water. Stir in sugar and set aside in a warm, draught-free place for 10 **minutes** or until mixture bubbles.

2. Combine flour, 1 **tsp** salt, sesame seeds, and cardamom in a large bowl. Add oil and yeast mixture, and mix to form a dough.

3. Turn dough out onto a lightly floured work surface and knead for 5 **minutes** or until smooth. Place in a lightly greased bowl, cover with plastic wrap, and set aside in a warm, draught-free place for 1 **hour** or until dough doubles in size.

4. Preheat oven to **180°C (355°F)**. Divide dough into two equal portions. Roll out to form two **30-cm** rounds (**12 inches**). Place into two greased **30-cm** skillets. Using a sharp knife, score 3 concentric circles in each round, working from the middle, out; then make 4 shallow cuts intersecting through the center to form a wheel pattern.

5. Brush with oil and bake for **20 minutes** or until cooked through and golden. Brush with butter and serve with hummus, if desired.

BEER BRATS: HOW FOOD BRINGS FAMILY TOGETHER

BY **Emily Lemmenes**

What I love most is when family gathers together after having not seen each other for some time, especially when food is involved. The Bible often talks about breaking bread together in fellowship. It's described as a practice of worship. What better way to catch up with loved ones than around the table? Every August on a hot summer day, my Illinois family joins together with its Wisconsin family to eat good food and reconnect with each other. One thing we always eat at family gatherings is bratwurst. Although my great-grandparents immigrated to Wisconsin from the Netherlands, they quickly adopted at least one piece of the predominantly German culture. By 1900, just fifty-two years into statehood, over two-hundred thousand German immigrants had settled in the Wisconsin area in hopes of developing inexpensive farmland. The bratwurst came along with them. We fell in line, too.

Sausages originated in the colder regions of Europe because they could be stored during the winter. Though the bratwurst ("fried sausage") originates from Germany, it was not until the Germans came to Wisconsin that the beer brat became a thing. Wisconsin adopted brewing at about the same time as the lumber industry settled in the state: hard-working lumbermen quickly became thirsty lumbermen.

Breweries were established in some small Wisconsin towns and eventually began growing throughout the state. This is still reflected in the baseball team, whose mascot is not the "Cubs" or "Tigers" or "Cardinals" but simply the "Brewers." It's no wonder the beer brat grew up here.

Every August, four brothers, my father included, along with their cousins and my grandfather join around the grill and cook up beer brats. The event used to take place once a year at a lake house ten miles south of the famous Sheboygan Brat Fest. Since my grandfather has gotten older, the event is now held at a nearby park so he doesn't have to host us at his house. The day is usually spent under the hot August sun, celebrating time together by swimming in Lake Michigan, playing beach volleyball, laughing together, and eating lots of bratwurst.

Driving up to the reunion has been a family tradition since I can remember. As a little girl, that ride seemed to take so long, though it probably only lasted about two and a half hours, three if we grew hungry or needed to stretch our legs. I just wanted to see my cousin Jessica, the girl cousin who was my age and would be just as excited to see me. But from an early age I have also enjoyed watching my father and uncles grill bratwurst. I remember sitting on the picnic table listening to my father and his brothers catch up over grilling. The conversations usually included stories about work, throwback stories from when they were young boys, and eventually the upcoming year for the Bears and Packers. I enjoyed watching my father, especially because he was always so happy around them. I know that he wished he could see his brothers more.

Today, the moment I smell a bratwurst, I begin to replay memories in my head of fifty family members gathered around a picnic table with cold beers in the hands of those who were of age and lots of laughter. The aroma of a beer brat is sweet and garlicky simultaneously. By the time mouths are watering and stomachs begin to growl, the bratwurst is served on a warm bun with the beer mixture added as a topping. I often forget that this is part of a German heritage when we're all eating our bratwursts together.

Prayer was always taken seriously in my family. As soon as the barbequers brought the food inside, before we could even grab a plate, my grandfather always made sure to say grace. I remember being impatient as I stood in the kitchen, listening to my grandfather pray for what seemed like five to ten minutes. Eventually, my stomach could not take it anymore and I would open my eyes and see the bratwurst sitting on the table, along with warm garlic potatoes and steamy creamed corn. Next to them would be the desserts. My mouth would water for some of my mother's dirt cake, a favorite among the younger ones. I would always make sure I was the first one in line to grab my food when my grandfather was finished praying. Something about waiting for five extra minutes after my dad and uncles had brought the food inside always made my appetite stronger.

There is something very comforting about sitting around the table with family while eating a meal you all enjoy. For that moment in time, the only thing we worried about was if there were going to be enough bratwursts for seconds, or even thirds. Conversations sprang up, and before you knew it, you could hardly hear the person across the table. But that was the way we liked it. Stories were told and memories were shared about my cousins and me. We all just laughed and enjoyed time together.

Food brings back memories and bratwurst brings

back some of the best memories for me and my family. Memories are a good thing to cherish because things never do remain exactly the same.

• • •

BEER BRATWURST

INGREDIENTS

6 bratwurst sausages

6 cups lager beer

2 large onions, sliced (divided)

1 Tbsp olive oil

2 red or green bell peppers, cored and sliced

Salt and freshly ground black pepper

6 bratwurst buns or hoagie rolls, split lengthwise

DIRECTIONS

1. Combine the bratwurst, beer, and half the onions. Simmer for about **15 minutes** or until bratwurst are firm and cooked through. Move the bratwurst from a pot to a plate. Keep the liquid that the bratwurst was cooked in.

2. Meanwhile, in a larger skillet, heat the oil over medium-high heat. Add the remaining onions and the bell peppers. Cook about **15 minutes** or until very soft, tossing occasionally. Add the bratwurst to the skillet in the last five minutes of cooking to lightly brown. If the vegetables begin to get too dark, add a few tablespoons of the bratwurst cooking liquid. Season to taste with salt and black pepper.

A NON-TRADITIONAL THANKSGIVING

BY Melanie Wolf

I hear the garage door shiver open from my bed, and I rise, rubbing the sleep from my eyes. I trek to the kitchen and almost instinctively spoon coffee grounds and cinnamon into the mouth of the coffee maker. Only then do I check, once, twice, three times, for the presence of a filter. I feel the familiar crinkle of the white paper and breathe a sigh of relief. Too often in my 6:45 a.m. slumber have I poured coffee grounds through the machine and onto the floor. I hear beeping both from the coffee maker starting and from the keypad on the door.

As shoes are kicked off and greetings made, I gather the dry ingredients: flour, sugar, baking powder, salt, and, most importantly, cinnamon. At this stage, there are three sets of hands working in the kitchen. This is when the song and dance begin. A cacophony of choreographed chaos rings through the house. Music plays from the counter, dishes clang together, cabinets open and shut, stomachs growl angrily, elbows bump together in the race to finish the meal. I incorporate the liquid ingredients into the dry, my whisk carelessly tossing batter into the air and onto the counter, floor, and sink. My Tia gives me a familiar look, asking herself, "Why do I let her in my kitchen?" Eggs are fried behind me as I do my usual routine of cleaning pancake batter off the cabinets. I hear the staccato spray of coconut oil onto a hot pan; smooth batter poured onto the sizzling oil makes a familiar, inviting sound. The moisture from the washed blueberries clashes with the hot oil in a series of pops, giving the song of the stove a percussive flair. I jump back into the flow of the busy kitchen, flipping pancakes and plating food as it finishes.

The first pancake (and sometimes the second) is the "sample pancake." This started as a method to gauge what needed to be added to the batter but soon became an excuse to have a pre-meal snack. I cannot remember a time that this did not result in the three of us burning our tongues from the excitement of tasting the fresh pancakes, running around with mouths wide open, trying to cool the food before swallowing it. At the snacking stage, the food is nearly done, begging to be consumed.

Two people remain in the kitchen, cleaning the surfaces and washing the last few dishes; one sets the table and brings the essential toppings: syrup, fruit, and salsa (for the eggs). We sit, already salivating at the sight and smells of the steaming plates. Arms reach across the table, fingers inviting the hands of the person adjacent. "With this hand, I give you my love," we say with a squeeze of the palm. We go around the table and give thanks for the food, for each other, and for our blessings. Not wasting any time, knives slide across the plates and toppings are added plentifully. The first bite of food is paralleled with the first morsel of conversation: a simple, "How was your night at work?" This quickly leads us to tangents upon tangents, jumping from "It was all right," to, "Remember that time we went to Petrified Forest? Was that in Arizona or New Mexico?" to, "Your grandma made me stop for ice cream at every single Dairy Queen we passed on the way out of

Texas." We laugh, and sometimes cry, finding comfort in a stack of cinnamon-laced pancakes.

I live in a third-shift household. Soon after I wake up and start my day, my family comes home and ends theirs. This makes breakfast the best time to spend time together in the kitchen and to break bread and reconnect, as opposed to eating dinner together. The food, though tasty, is but a vehicle for reconnection and conversation. We have our most treasured conversations at breakfast, anywhere from a lighthearted talk about how miserable the weather is to our deepest conversations about our future and purpose in this world. Though breakfast is not traditionally a celebratory meal, my family and I have grown to show appreciation for each other daily, to celebrate the time we have been given together. The overwhelming scents of cinnamon and coffee are the scents I associate with a "Thanksgiving" meal, and I wouldn't have it any other way.

. . .

ARISMENDEZ-WOLF PANCAKES

INGREDIENTS

1 **cup** almond milk

2 **Tbsps** unsalted butter, melted

1 large egg

2 **tsps** vanilla extract

1 **cup** all-purpose flour

2½ **Tbsps** sugar

2 **tsps** baking powder

½ **tsp** salt

Cinnamon, to taste

Coconut oil cooking spray

Blueberries (optional)

DIRECTIONS

1. Combine almond milk, melted butter, egg, and vanilla extract in one bowl.

2. Combine flour, sugar, baking powder, salt, and cinnamon in another.

3. Slowly incorporate the wet and dry ingredients, not overmixing. Optional: Fold blueberries into batter; do not crush.

4. Heat medium-sized pan on medium-high, spray coconut oil for half a second onto surface of pan, and pour batter to desired pancake size.

5. Flip when golden brown and cook other side. Serve
   with butter and syrup.

MY MOTHER'S FAMOUS CORN PUDDING RECIPE

BY Julia Belcher

It is Thanksgiving evening, better known in my family as the night before Black Friday, a holiday we all take very seriously. The air outside is frigid cold and a light snow is falling, covering the ground. It is late at night, as family gatherings always go with us, and the moon outside is shining bright, reflecting an eerie glow off the fallen snow. All the women gather around the dining room table with glasses of warm apple cider and magazines with large, colorful ads announcing upcoming Black Friday deals. It has been a tradition for as long as I have been alive, and I'm sure even years before that. Black Friday is an important part of my family's Thanksgiving, the planning and the decisions of where to go and what to buy are like a game to us, and something we enjoy doing as a family every year.

Sitting around the large wooden table with my family, my stomach full, finding all the good deals of Black Friday, is one of my favorite family memories. Even if the kitchen is always several degrees warmer than the rest of the house, I find it is the best place to be, enjoying the time with my cousins, sister, aunts, mom and grandma, satisfied with the environment. It is full of my family, my favorite people, the smells in the air, the food all around. The fresh baked bread, the Thanksgiving turkey, the stuffing, and even the pumpkin pie were prepared in the same kitchen, taking hard hours of preparation and cooking. Afterwards all the women gather to finish the dishes we have been working on all day. Some of the preparation may have been done at home, but eventually all the families make it to my grandma's house to finish preparing their meals together.

"Julia, get the rolls out of the oven," my grandmother says, shouting across the noise of the kitchen.

"Watch Out! Hot pan!" "Turn the stove down, don't let that pot boil over!" "Cut up the fruit!" Voices fill the air as my family members run and shout across the kitchen, all rushing to make sure the food is finished perfectly, and on time.

Things around me seem to go in slow motion. Despite the detailed movements of people rushing around, moving at such a fast pace, my mind can slow everything down. I am surrounded by all of my favorite things. I love the upcoming season of holidays, blessed by family and good food. For Thanksgiving in particular, I love being able to stand in the kitchen, watching it fill with delicious foods, especially my mother's corn pudding.

In my family, especially, everyone knows the most important part of the Thanksgiving meal isn't the turkey, but all the side dishes. Other families may have their own favorite, but my favorite, and the favorite of everyone else in my family, is my mom's corn pudding. I can remember every year my younger brothers asking, "Mom, you're making your corn pudding this year, right?" and my mom would reassure them every year that she always would. The corn pudding recipe was one that was passed down from mother to daughter in my family and has been a family recipe for many, many years.

Corn pudding is a typical southern food, and has

actually been in America since the Native Americans prepared it thousands of years ago. Native Americans would take fresh corn, water, and the milky residue left over from scraping the kernels off the cobs. The ingredients were then baked in a pot until the starch in the corn thickened the mixture. When Europeans learned how to make this dish from Native Americans, they eventually worked in ingredients such as milk, eggs, cream and butter, to look more like the traditional dish we eat today. This dish has been passed down for many years in my family, descendants of European settlers, and is part of the important family home-cooked meals that I miss very much. It reminds me of my Southern heritage and all the Southern food that I love. My mom made sure we were a family that always ate together, waiting for everyone in the family to arrive home to eat. I can picture my mom standing over the stove, her hair tied back, steam surrounding her. Her hands move fast, as they know exactly what to do without her telling them. Some recipes she doesn't even need to look at. Corn pudding was a dish like that. She knew it by heart and had a passion for cooking it. I can recall it now, the taste of the warm corn pudding making my mouth water just thinking about it. The meaning behind the food, and the memories that tie in with the dish are just as important as the dish itself.

There have many changes throughout our family over the years. People grew up, there were fights and arguments. But people also came together, there were births, and moments of bonding. While many things changed, something we always knew we could count on being the same was the food. My family wanted certain recipes to be followed the same way, every time. Corn pudding was one of them. It should be made the exact same way following the exact same recipe as it had many years ago. While change is something that is good, over the years it is good to have something to hold the family together, even something as small and seemingly insignificant as food.

I love the stories that come at dinner time when the family is gathered around the table. I love the feeling of satisfaction as every one of us devours their favorite food, and feels a full stomach. I love the warm and familiar environment of being surrounded by my family, and the people I love, all of us bonding over my mother's corn pudding.

. . .

CORN PUDDING

INGREDIENTS

1 can cream corn

2 cans kernel corn, drained

1 (8-oz) sour cream

1 stick butter, melted

1 box Jiffy cornbread

2 eggs, beaten

DIRECTIONS

Mix all of the ingredients together and bake at 375°F for 40 minutes.

MY "SECRET" FAMILY RECIPE: OJ BANANA BREAD MUFFINS

BY Kelsie Thornell

In my family, we have very few traditions. We never do things exactly the same. Thanksgiving and Christmas are a little different every year, and this may be because we are disorganized. The one thing that did remain the same is the warm aroma of my mom's OJ banana bread muffins. We've had it ever since I was very young and anyone who tries it loves it.

Bananas have an interesting history. Originally from Southeast Asia, and studied as early as the fourth century B.C. by one of Aristotle's students, they never were popular in a rice-based diet. Banana bread also wasn't discovered until fairly late—not until the eighteenth century, when other "quick breads," breads baked without baking powder, were developed.

Banana bread first became popular in the United States during the time of the Great Depression. It likely made it into cookbooks during this time because it involves over-ripe bananas, which would not have been thrown away very quickly or easily during this time of economic crisis.

My family's history with banana bread started some time later, after they moved to the United States. During World War II my great-grandparents lived in the

Netherlands. One afternoon they heard a knock at their door. Standing in their doorway were members of the Dutch Underground looking for a place to hide some Jewish refugees. My grandparents felt quite nervous about this because of the huge risk involved, but they felt it was their duty as Christians to offer them a place to hide. These Jews lived with them and stayed deep within the interior of their home until my great-grandpa was asked to take on a greater responsibility.

At this time, the leader of the Dutch Underground had been captured and was being led on foot by Nazis down a country road. A man on a bicycle rode past them and the leader saw this as a great opportunity. When the bicyclist was next to them, the underground leader pushed the Nazis into the bike and was able to make his escape. But he of course had to go into hiding, which left a huge leadership role empty.

Shortly after this time, my great-grandpa was asked to take over the position of leader. He felt called to accept. This put him and his family at great risk, which resulted in my great-grandma taking my grandpa and his brother into the country to stay with relatives until the war was over. Unfortunately, Nazis found them out one night and knowing they were related to my great-grandpa emptied their entire house except for a plaque that was left standing on the wall. This plaque read, "Onze hulp staat en de naam van Heer die hemel en aarde gemaakt." In English, this translates to Psalm 124:8, "Our help is in the name of the Lord, who made heaven and earth." The Nazis found my grandpa hiding in the house and asked his cousins who he was. They said he was a neighbor. If they had told the truth that day, the soldiers would have taken my grandpa and I would not be writing this paper today, or even be here at all.

After World War II, my great-grandparents and their family immigrated to the U.S. to pursue better opportunities. During this period, they had very little money so they'd eat relatively cheap foods such as potatoes, corn, and bananas. Especially during the hot summer months in Michigan, their bananas and other produce would ripen very quickly. Because they didn't have much money, they used their over-ripe bananas to make banana bread.

Even after my great-grandpa started a fabric store and the family started to have more money, they still made the banana bread because it tasted so good. They even experimented by adding orange juice for the taste and sprinkling brown sugar on top. My grandma learned to make it by the time she married into the family and later, when the time came, my mom learned to make it, too.

My first experience with banana bread was in 2000, when I was four years old. One warm summer morning the aroma of bananas sweetened by sugar drew me to the kitchen, where I repeatedly asked my mom what she was making until she had the chance to answer me. She finally told me the name and then opened up the oven door, releasing intense heat into the air while placing the pan on top of the stove to cool.

For the next few minutes I waited as patiently as a four-year-old is able to until the muffins were cool enough to eat. The warm banana bread's smell filled my nose and increased my appetite by the minute. Finally, my mom scooped out a muffin and put it on a plate at the counter. I scrambled up the barstool and plopped myself down in front of the muffin. I hesitated for a moment, but as soon as the muffin's sweet flavor hit my tongue I experienced this new sensation of flavors I wasn't familiar with. I don't recall if I immediately grabbed another muffin from the cooling tin, but I believe that there is a good chance that I did.

Most people know what banana bread is, so it really isn't a very unique recipe, but the way my mom makes it is key to why it is so good. She makes the muffins perfectly moist so they aren't too dry but they also don't stick to your mouth when you eat them. The "secret" ingredient of orange juice really completes the taste of the muffins, too. I miss it when I eat a muffin made by someone other than my mom.

When I move into my own place someday and actually have to cook my own food, I will make sure to get the banana bread recipe from my mom. It is a family recipe that I will continue to share throughout the coming generations because these muffins are delicious, easy to make, and significant in my family's heritage.

• • •

"BANANA BREAD HISTORY."
Banana Bread. N.p., n.d. Web. 15 Sept. 2015.

"The Interesting Tale of Banana Bread History in America."
Botanical Journeys Plant Guides. N.p., n.d. Web. 03 Sept. 2015.

OJ BANANA BREAD MUFFINS

INGREDIENTS

1 **cup** sugar

2 **Tbsps** shortening

2 eggs

2 **cups** flour

1 **tsp** vanilla

½ **tsp** salt

1 **tsp** baking powder

1 **tsp** baking soda

2 large, ripe bananas

½ **cup** orange juice

DIRECTIONS

Preheat oven to **325°F.** Mash bananas and shortening together with fork in large mixing bowl. Mix with the rest of the ingredients with electric mixer, adding flour slowly. Pour into greased mini muffin tins or regular muffin tins. Top each muffin with a bit of brown sugar. Bake mini-sized muffins for **15** to **20 minutes,** or regular muffins for **20** to **25 minutes** (or until golden brown and not mushy on top).

VIETNAMESE PICKLED MUSTARD GREENS

BY ThiLanAnh Nguyen

"Don't touch it! Leave the duck alone!"

"They don't trust me," I murmur a couple times as I stomp out of Grandma's kitchen. Grandma, Mom, and Aunt Tuyet never allow me to stay around the kitchen, as I have a tendency to ruin things. Still, I wanted to stay.

Grandma, Mom, and Aunt Tuyet always fascinated me by their cooking talents. Each was a perfect combination of food chemist and culinary magician. Within two hours, raw duck, or occasionally chicken, still with white feathers; unprocessed mushrooms; carb claw herbs, still with soil clung to their roots; fresh cuttlefishes, bought for 5,000 đồng (a quarter), cheaper after Mom's five minutes of bargaining with the seafood vendor; tomatoes; and shallots would turn into delicious, aromatic dishes and be displayed exquisitely on Grandma's 22.6-inch radius table.

We would use that round dining table, with its delicate, bronze, curved Vietnamese patterns, almost every day. The table is usually placed across from Grandma's kitchen, right at the center of Grandma's garden. I sometimes daydreamed and was late for school as I stared aimlessly at Grandma's phloxes, orchids, and frangipani while having my favorite breakfast: *bun man* (rice vermicelli with boiled pork slices, fermented pork roll, peanuts, chopped papaya, and a special sauce with fermented fish, sugar, and pineapple). Although I hate fish in general, *bun man*, fried tuna, and sour soup are three fish-related foods that Mom doesn't have to waste her time forcing me to eat.

"Go do your homework, and don't try to finger these dried mustard greens with your unwashed hands." Mom tried to send me her last warning before I would disappear from her sight.

"They still don't believe in me," I muttered while heading to Grandma's garden. Her flowers would certainly appease my frustration with being expelled. It was 100 degrees Fahrenheit. The sun was burning my scalp. I found a rainbow-colored folding bed in Uncle Luc's storage room. To a seven-year-old girl, nothing was greater than lying on Uncle Luc's folding bed, facing Grandma's guava canopies, and pretending that I had the super power to shoot down some bittersweet and watery, yet seedy, guavas.

Sun streaks slanting through the guava leaves woke me up.

I was seven years old.

Summer breeze lifted the symphony of crickets and "L'amour Est Bleu" and lingered on Grandma's garden. As it was moving, the zephyr accidentally carried countless phlox particles that powerfully evoked my memories of the age of seven. I was still in Grandma's garden, but this time I was ten. Aunt Tuyet was chopping some chili peppers. The chopping rhythm was exactly the one I had heard when I was seven, lilting and mellifluous. Wind, phloxes, cricket and chopping sounds all were present, yet an important thing was missing. I missed Grandma and her pickled mustard greens.

"Na (my nickname at home), you need to understand

that these are for Uncle Ngoc's guests. Next time, you can help if there is no guest. I want our guests to have a good time at our home." Mom approached Uncle Luc's folding bed, where I sulkily lay, and explained the reason for yelling at me when I had tried to touch the crabs that were crawling around Grandma's aluminum sink. I was very fond of watching the crabs make their way up the sink's margin and then pushing them back into the sink. Mom gave me a tiny boiled chicken egg she found—after making a sagittal cut of a boiled chicken's abdomen—as an apology. The egg didn't taste better than normal eggs, smaller and harder to bite through, but it was enough to cheer me up as a lucky sign.

I was still untrustworthy even after I became a little older. The adults would allow me to organize bowls, dishes, and napkins before Uncle Ngoc's guests came, but still they would say, "Don't touch it!" when it came to the food.

I suddenly heard a familiar shrill of metals; somebody had just arrived home. Grandma's metallic door always creates an unpleasant sound when someone tries to open it. We usually joke that Grandma's door can be used as a security guard to protect us from theft. Uncle Luc walked through the door with a bag full of ice and sodas. One of Grandma's home traditions is to drink wine, tea, and water only. My brother and I were always happy to drink wine if allowed. Sadly, Uncle Luc's sodas were for us. In the next fifteen minutes, that metallic shrill repeated itself a couple times. Dad, Uncle Nhat, and Uncle Ngoc and his guests had arrived.

Soon after, chats and greetings filled up Grandma's house with a fresh kind of energy that I hadn't seen after Grandma passed away when I was nine. After ten minutes of waiting for the food to be displayed on Grandma's round table, the guests quickly took their seats. Uncle Ngoc, who is a priest, started the feast by prayer. I normally felt uneasy while staying quietly on my seat and waiting for the prayer to finish, as I always felt the orange-steamed shrimps, one of my family's traditional foods, kept inviting me to dip them into Mom's creamy handmade mayonnaise sauce or Aunt Tuyet's *muoi tieu* (a sour and salty sauce). That day was an exception. My mouth didn't even salivate. I missed Grandma.

After the prayer ended, Uncle Luc turned on his cassette, which, I bet, was part of my family even before my brother was born. As the cassette started to play Kenny G's collection, the clink from wine glasses opened the feast. The shrimps and cuttlefishes were still steaming. Chicken congee's greasy surface, originating from the chicken's fat, gleamed under the ceiling lights. A plate of mixed home-grown vegetables with tomato sauce were my chopsticks' main target. Chicken was chopped in parallelogram pieces and arranged neatly on Grandma's two biggest plates to facilitate the distribution of food.

Mom gave me a mayonnaise-dipped shrimp. Sweetness started at the tip of my tongue, filled up my mouth, and spread all the way down to my stomach as I first bit half of the shrimp. The shrimp's juice that was carefully conserved by different levels of fire during the cooking process burst in my mouth. Crispy vegetables created a merry sound joined with someone's laughter. People talked about anything: politics, jobs, and family. A woman asked Mom her secret in choosing good shrimp after giving praises to the food. I tried to finish my dishes as fast as possible to betake myself to Grandma's bed. Partly, I was aware that the adults might ask about my studying, one of the adults' favorite topics. Partly, I missed Grandma and her homemade pickled mustard greens as a guest exclaimed that it had been a year since Grandma's funeral.

Pickled mustard greens filled my early childhood since that was the only thing I ate with rice and soybean sauce almost every day. Before I turned six, Grandma's family was poor. Grandpa was MIA, so Grandma took the responsibility of raising five kids on her own. Even when I was born, the economy was not much better than when Grandma first received the news that Grandpa was MIA. Rice was still an expensive thing to have. Grandma usually bought cheap fresh mustard greens from the market that was 500 meters away from her house. She then would remove rotten parts of mustard greens and always double checked before recycling the unwanted parts for fertilization. My family learned to value food from her. Grandma had a big clay jar that was used to pickle dried, chopped mustard greens with diluted salt and shallots. The shallots and mustard greens' acridity would sometimes run up to my brain when I first opened the jar. The adults would sometimes help Grandma with pickling if they didn't have to work. My brother and I were too little to help with carrying that big clay jar. "Don't touch it!" Grandma would say. I always found a contradiction whenever I saw my 4'9" Grandma carry a jar that was almost a third of her height. I was too little to understand that whenever the adults said, "I'm full," it was to save rice for my brother and me. They, instead, ate steamed cassavas. I loved having rice during winter and rainy days. The moment of opening the rice cooker's lid was the most exciting. Steam would sally out and warm up my face. I sometimes would think of the steam as my prayer to God for giving us food and hope it would go up to the sky. My family's surviving off of Grandma's pickled mustard greens explains the reason for my love of sour food.

Now, I'm here, in the United States for almost two years, eating many kinds of good dishes. I still eat pickled mustard greens made by Mom. Mom has learned to make different foods with pickled mustard greens: greens sour soup, round scad stew with greens, fried greens with bacon, and so on. However, Grandma's pickled mustard greens with warmed rice and soybean sauce is still irreplaceable. I miss Grandma and the country that I've been far away from for two years. Part of me is still in Vietnam, calling the other parts to come home.

• • •

VIETNAMESE PICKLED MUSTARD GREENS

INGREDIENTS

1 Tbsp salt

2 lbs shallots

1 tsp sugar

½ lb mustard greens, steamed, cut into **1-inch** pieces

DIRECTIONS

1. Combine **2 cups** of water, salt, and sugar in a saucepan over medium heat, and bring to a boil. Remove from heat.

2. Pack the chopped mustard greens into a **1-quart** jar and pour in the brine. When the greens are cool and turn to a pale yellow, they are ready.

3. Cover and refrigerate for up to a week. Drain the greens before eating.

HOMEMADE: BONDING OVER DUTCH BANKET

BY Catherine Van Lonkhuyzen

Stepping from under the hidden shadows of the overhang, I'm bathed in the warm sun of September. The hustle of those around me, and trying to keep up with my father, contrasts the sun rays that flow down from the whimsical clouds above. We step into the stream of fellow Dutchmen and women, who in some way from decades ago, we are probably related to. The heat is oppressive, but also comforting in the idea of the cold Chicago winter to come. My father and I swim through the crowd, until we reach our destination. We slow down at the entrance to the food tent of the Elim Dutch Festival of Crestwood but, once inside, immediately spot what we are looking for against the opposite wall: the few bars of banket that have survived the morning rush. We grab as many as our arms can hold, and rush to the cashier. On our way home, I look down at the Delft blue plastic bag on my lap. This small taste will satisfy a winter, spring, and summer-long craving, and yet it still won't be the same. As delightful as these frozen batches can be, I can't help but be reminded of the previous December, when copious amounts of warm, fresh, homemade banket, were lined up in a row on the center island of my aunt's kitchen at the Van Lonkhuyzen Christmas Party.

As we take off our winter boots, tiny snowflakes fall to the rug at the front door of my Aunt Sandy's house, adding to the wet and muddy pool already forming. December has only just begun, but the shadows of a long and brutal winter have already begun to creep into every home. We can already hear faint snippets of conversation taking place in the living room as Uncle Jerry comes to greet us. Family members are already scattered across the whole living room. More are in the kitchen, chatting with a glass of punch in hand, as they eagerly await the oven timer to sound. The rest are strewn across two couches, the heater, an archaic small wooden stool, and several dining room chairs that have been pulled over from the other side of the room to join the conversation.

As my mom places our contribution to the family dinner on the kitchen counter with the other tinfoil-wrapped pans, the Tupperware, and the steaming crock-pots, I sit down on my Aunt Sandy's far too soft couch next to my grandmother. She is the matriarch of my family, and always, without fail, is the first one to arrive. At the age of 97, every other person in the room can thank her for their being here. My cousin Dan is telling of his latest hunting adventure. Then he makes sure to remind us that, "there's deer sausage in the kitchen if anyone wants it." Then my cousin Lisa comes with her kids. Abby immediately comes to me with her new fiancé, now husband, and asks me if I'm still going into nursing. She recently graduated as a nurse, and is eager to show me all the tips and tricks I'll need to survive.

As more and more cousins, grandkids, uncles, and aunts pour in, Aunt Sandy shouts across the chaos that dinner is finally ready. Immediately the room becomes silent. Keeping with tradition, my dad prays over the food and over our family of sixty. At the sound of "Amen," the plates are passed around and the pots uncovered to let the warm steam of the homemade dishes rise to warm our cold December faces. I usually wait until the stampede has died down before grabbing a plate for my grandma and me. It's the same every year: the cheesy potato casserole that spent too much time in the oven, the slow roasted turkey that's been bathing in the hot water of a crock pot, and of course the deer sausage. Dinner is more of a formality—something to get over with as we wait for the desserts to be set out. As everyone sits down to eat, the whole house becomes the dining room table. Coffee tables, stairs, the slouchy couches, the kitchen island, and even the floor become packed with family members, sprawled out and discussing what's happened over the previous year. Each year we ask my grandma how she likes the food, and each year she replies with a radiant smile and, "It's *so* good!" My grandmother's love for all types of food has always inspired and delighted me, because she knows the value of a good meal and good company.

Conversations usually drift backwards to when my dad, my aunts, and my uncle Curt were young. By now, the kids have been sent downstairs to watch a movie so that the adults can relax and enjoy their meals. I remember feeling so accomplished when I graduated from the basement to the upstairs. Soon, the leftovers are divided into plates to take home, and the desserts are set out to be crammed into the oven. Along with the other desserts, the long awaited banket is taken out of the freezer where it's been waiting all day. Baked fresh in the morning, the banket now is lifted from its frigid spot to the oven, captivating an audience of longing and patient eyes in the kitchen and dining room. This is when everyone begins to get antsy.

As we patiently wait for the goodies to come, all the chairs and benches scattered around the room are brought into the family room and placed in a circle. Now the games begin. Our whole family gathers around the pile of mysteriously wrapped presents on the center coffee table to play a massive game of White Elephant. Each year, someone sneaks a greatly desired sausage and cheese sampler into the mix, which causes the game to get rather violent. It gets passed around from family to family until it can't be stolen any longer, to the cries and groans of all my uncles. The game always ends in roaring laughter and apologies. After the game, my grandma passes out the Dutch chocolate letters to everyone in my family—another Dutch tradition we hold dear. Over the years, as the number of members of our family has grown, the box she brings to the Christmas party has grown as well. No one is ever left out.

Soon, warm and buttery scents waft from the kitchen to our eager noses. This is the moment we've been waiting for. We all gather in the tiny kitchen as the oven door is carefully opened. Heavenly smells fill the whole house. Anticipation strikes the heart. This is our definition of Christmastime.

Banket is traditionally made in the Netherlands as a Christmas treat. It's made with pastry dough that is rolled out and filled with thick blocks of almond paste that are baked into the middle. Though banket seems like the Dutch version of American Christmas cookies left out for Santa, banket is simply a treat meant to be enjoyed among family members. Dutch children will lay carrots and oats in their wooden shoes and leave them outside the front door for Sinterklaas' horse to enjoy when Sinterklaas is leaving presents. I'm sure Sinterklaas' horse would prefer banket instead.

Willing hands reach out and set the rows of homemade banket onto the counter to cool. Sometimes we can't even wait that long, so a line forms from the kitchen all the way to the front door. The other pies and homemade goods are brought out as well, but everyone knows what dish is going to disappear first. Made by my Aunt Sandy with my grandma's own recipe, the banket has the perfect buttery, golden brown layers on the outside, with warm, gooey almond paste on the inside. The perfect match between crunchy and soft. The delicately rolled layers melt in my mouth, revealing the present of sweet and sticky goodness. There is nothing that speaks more to me about home and heritage than banket. No matter how far our enormous family wanders, we are never too far to be brought home. We are all connected through our devotion to our heritage and each other, even though we only see each other once a year.

As we bump along home, nearing the small hill that rolls down to our driveway, I finger the blue plastic bag on my lap. It will still be gobbled up within a week. It will still have the familiar and comforting flavors of buttery crust and sugary almond tang. The memories that come back to me are almost as comforting as the flavors themselves. It may not be homemade, but it reminds me of home.

• • •

BANKET

INGREDIENTS

2 **cups** all-purpose flour

1 **cup** butter

½ **cup** water

1½ **cups** almond paste

2 eggs

¾ **cup** white sugar

¼ **tsp** almond extract (or vanilla, whatever is preferred)

1 **pinch** salt

1 egg white, beaten

DIRECTIONS

1. In a large bowl, cut cold butter or margarine into flour until the mixture has a crumb-like texture. Make a well in the center, then add cold water. Mix together until the mixture forms a ball. Do not over mix. Chill dough.

2. Preheat oven to **450°F.** Grease cookie sheets.

3. In a medium bowl, blend together almond paste, eggs, ¾ **cup** sugar, almond extract and salt.

4. Divide dough into 4 parts, and roll into **15-inch** strips. Place filling along the center of each long strip of dough. Roll up, and pinch the ends to seal. Take a fork and poke holes on top of the roll, **2 inches** apart, to vent. Place strips **2 inches** apart on cookie sheet. Brush with egg white, and sprinkle with the remaining sugar.

5. Bake for **15** to **20 minutes**, or until golden.

TRADITION IS MORE THAN JUST FOR FAMILY

BY Allyson Kranstz

Growing up in Michigan meant cold winters, frozen fingers, and mugs of hot chocolate. It's said that the feeling of holding a hot mug mimics the warmth emitted from holding the hand of another human being. This is why on a cold dark night, a mug of cocoa is all you need to relax. While family traditions are typically thought of as shared with those who share your blood, family to me are those I love, who love me, and with whom I share homemade hot chocolate on a freezing cold night after blazing down a mountain going thirty miles an hour.

Thursday nights for the past five years in winter have meant one thing and one thing only to me: ski club. My friends got me into skiing in the eighth grade and ever since I have been hooked. I remember the first time my mother took me to a ski swap at our local ski resort, Timber Ridge, to buy the equipment I would need for the following winter. Ski swaps take place in the musty, damp lodge where people can buy and sell anything from skis and snowboards to poles and gloves. Knowing almost nothing about skiing at the time I picked out skis in a color I liked, found my size for boots and was on my way. Right from the start, I had to get used to the customs. The night would go as follows: once I got to Timber Ridge I bought my lift ticket, found the reserved table and put my bag on the chair I'd claim as my own, put my gear on, and went outside to ski. After a few hours of carving the quad and the black diamond, I'd eventually come to an agreement with my friends to head in and eat. No one brings their phone out on the slopes so the passing of time is dictated by how frozen your lips and nose get, the cool brisk air calling for something warm, something with more flavor than the ice that collects on your teeth. The lodge has carpeted floors and when people come in, the snow melts onto the old, moldy floor and the smell isn't something you'd like to stay with you. All it took was a few steps towards our table until my nostrils filled with the promising aroma of homemade dishes. Each week a different family would prepare and bring a meal for the kids who were going to be skiing that Thursday. The Forster family always brought a savory and sweet BBQ pulled pork dish served with some vegetables and chips for the side; the Ashmore's, a potato casserole with cheese that strings from your lips to the plate. The Stolstkey's always had homemade pumpkin bread for dessert, with more spice than you'd think necessary, but your taste buds told you otherwise. Each week a new meal was served and I would grow increasingly eager for Thursday night, when I knew there'd be something delicious to have for dinner.

While the food filled our stomachs and gave us energy for more rounds on the hills until the park would shut down, what warmed me the most was the Snowden's fresh-made hot chocolate. Every Thursday I could expect my friend Allison, who, ironically enough, we call Snow, to bring the both of us a thermos of her mom's hot chocolate. Each sip of the thick, fudge-like drink sent waves of heat all the way down my throat into my stomach. Snow and I would go out together, her snowboarding, me skiing, and every single night we'd both ask to go in for hot chocolate at the same time. We knew when it was time for a break, time to get warm. While the snow melted off our hats and gloves, the drink would warm us up so much we'd end up taking off our coats and sometimes even our snow pants. Her mom would make it fresh on the stove before Snow came to ski club. She always knew I liked more milk in mine than Snow, making a separate batch just for me, a special treat for our hard work that day. After falls and wipeouts, beautiful carves and hockey-like stops, after conversations on the ski lift over the dim hum of the conveyor belt, I knew I could count on an industrial grade thermos to keep the cocoa hot until needed.

As we sipped from the black and grey metal canisters we'd sit by the cold glass windows and comment on the other skiers on the hills, critiquing style and skill. "His coat and pants don't match," I'd say and Snow would respond with a comment about how it's not about looks, but about technique on the turns or the speed at which they could keep control that makes a good skier, but I always matched my gear, not because it made me look better, but because it'd bug me if I didn't match. Snow would wear her blue and white coat with green camo snow pants and a black helmet, but she was a better snowboarder than I so I rarely made a comment about it. At the window table in the lodge we could find our friends on the lift or coming down the hill. We got good at finding the unique coats of our group. When our cups started to run low we'd have a contest: first one to find three of our friends won and the loser had to chug the now semi-warm cocoa in five seconds. After an incident involving the hot chocolate on my white coat, the window, and the carpet in the lodge, we decided that five seconds was too quick. On particularly cold nights I'd lose the competition on purpose just to feel the warm rush of chocolate run down my throat, sparking a small fire in the pit of my stomach.

Everyone in our group understood the unspoken rule that the cocoa was only for me and Snow. While the occasional sip was asked for, the rest of the club was provided another drink, usually pop or water, and those who really wanted something else would supply their own. Snow's mom made it for us and us alone. She made it so often she never had to write down how much sugar or cocoa was needed, never had a recipe in front of her. She developed the combination on her own and ever since I started skiing with Snow it has only been shared with me. To Snow it's another drink on a wintery night, delicious, yes, but it's always been a part of her life, her mother making it since she was little. To me the hot chocolate is more than that. It makes me part of her family, at least a little. It's something that I could look forward to sharing with a friend no matter what happened that week. There was a sense of reliability in the thermos brought each Thursday. It was a reminder that more than just your parents and siblings can love you, because her mother perfecting the amount of milk that I enjoyed, just the right amount of vanilla, showed me that she wanted it to be right, she wanted it to be just right for me. It's a simple recipe, but the love added into it, from someone who isn't related to me, is what makes it so rich.

• • •

HOT COCOA

INGREDIENTS

1 **cup** sugar

3 **Tbsps** cocoa

3½ **cups** milk

1½ **tsps** vanilla

DIRECTIONS

1. Place pot on stove
2. Stir sugar and cocoa
3. Add milk slowly, whisking the whole time
4. Add vanilla as you take it off the burner
5. Based on taste, add more milk or not

YOUNG YANG BAB: NUTRITIOUS RICE

BY Yuseon (Ellen) Lee

It was a beautiful sunny day in fall; the humid and hot air of summer had gone, and cool winds accompanied sunny days. The relatives on my mother's side had gathered to have dinner together. My mom was hanging out with her sister, and once they start to talk it usually lasts for hours. My sister, who is older than I, tried to join their conversation, but I thought it was a little boring. My grandmother was in the kitchen, making her special food by herself. She always makes a meal called *Young Yang Bab*, which means "Nutritious Rice."

While all the adults of my family, including my mom, dad, aunts, and grandfather, loved *Young Yang Bab* and waited for it eagerly, my siblings and I hated it. I always picked out the chestnuts, which were the only thing I liked, and whined to my mom about the rest. She would suggest that I try at least one spoonful, often telling me, "Someday you will miss this too." I never thought she would be right, but I do kind of miss it now. I guess that's because I miss my grandmother.

My grandmother got the recipe from her mother when she lived in Icheon, a province in South Korea famous for its high quality rice. She mixed the rice with ingredients such as Job's tears, red beans, ginkgo nuts, and jujubes to make sure we would all get enough calcium and vitamins to stay healthy. For the children who didn't like to eat harsh grains and beans, grandmother would roll the rice with a seaweed sheet like a roll cake, because my siblings and I loved seaweed.

My grandmother was a great cook, but once she started to worry about our family's health, she created some weird food. One time, my grandmother got some strange white powder, mixed it with some milk, and fermented it for about a week. This made a kind of sticky white liquid that looked like yogurt but smelled like vomit. She offered it to my brother, who was weak at the time with rhinitis and anemia, and caused a game of cat-and-mouse between them.

The food I hated most was "carp soup." When my grandmother boiled carp, the house would fill with a strange stench, and all of the children in my family, including me, would start to shiver with fear. Compared to these, we liked *Young Yang Bab*, though we certainly never said so.

Sometimes when we begged my grandfather not to make us eat *Young Yang Bab*, he would tell us an old story about a mother-in-law and daughter-in-law who were on bad terms. The mother-in-law didn't like the daughter-in-law and abused her, so the daughter-in-law decided to get rid of her. She went to a shaman and asked how this could be done. The shaman told her to put ten chestnuts in her rice every day for one hundred days. These would fatten and eventually kill her mother-in-law. The daughter-in-law did just that, faithfully putting ten chestnuts in the rice for one hundred days. However, instead of making her fat, the chestnuts only made the mother-in-law healthier. In the end, the mother-in-law became so healthy that she felt sorry for being mean to her daughter-in-law and decided to be kind to her instead. Soon the two became friends.

At the end of his story, my grandfather would grin and say, "Can you imagine a conflict between a mother-in-law and a daughter-in-law could be resolved just by rice? If only it were so easy." I think he said that because my grandmother and my aunt didn't always get along. My aunt lived on Jeju Island, a beautiful island full of wind, volcanic rock, and mandarins. One year, we had to visit Jeju Island to see some of our family members who were sick. My siblings and I fell in love with the island. We saw a beautiful harmony between the great number of yellow canola blossoms that grew there and the black basalt rock face. We ate my aunt's special *Young Yang Bab*, which she took pride in cooking. She had a restaurant in downtown Seogwipo, and to attract guests, she used natural pigments like canola blossoms and purple cactus to tint her rice. Then she put chestnuts, mushrooms, and green ginkgo nuts on it. We could tell she was absorbed in the beauty of her cooking.

Though my parents were always impressed by the beauty of my aunt's dishes, my grandmother disapproved of them. She said it was a waste of time since it took a day to tint the rice yellow. A good cook's focus should be nutrition, not the color of her rice. My grandmother also did not care for the fact that my aunt spoke in the dialect of Jeju. As Jeju Island is far from the peninsula of Korea, its dialect sounds like another language to many Koreans. My grandmother had a very hard time trying to understand what my aunt was saying, and she thought my aunt was being purposefully obscure.

Even if what they focused on was totally different, both my grandmother's and my aunt's versions of *Young Yang*

Bab show how much they valued their family. To them, this food was more than just a bowl of rice. It was a demonstration of how much they loved us. Now that I'm living away from home, I would like to mix together both my aunt's and my grandmother's versions of *Young Yang Bab*. Why not make it both healthy and beautiful? If I have a chance to make *Young Yang Bab*, I want to tint the rice with canola blossoms and then mix that up with lots of grains and beans. I would like to show my friends in America my gratefulness for their warm reception by making them my own recipe. To make *Young Yang Bab*, I have to put all my effort into making this rice as my grandmother and my aunt did.

• • •

YOUNG YANG BAB

INGREDIENTS

Rice

Canola oil

Sweet pumpkin

Job's tears

Red beans

Ginkgo nuts

Jujubes

Ginseng

Chestnuts

Sweet potatoes

Rice

Seaweed

Flowers

SAUCE INGREDIENTS

Soy sauce

Pepper powder

Garlic, diced

Sesame seeds

Sesame oil

continued

DIRECTIONS

1. Soak rice in canola oil for a day.

2. Chop a sweet pumpkin into small pieces.

3. Soak Job's tears and ginkgo nuts in water.

4. Fry ginkgo nuts.

5. Boil red beans.

6. Chop some jujubes, chestnuts and sweet potatoes into small pieces with ginseng.

7. Cook the yellow rice with chopped pumpkins, Job's tears, fried ginkgo nuts, boiled red beans, jujubes, ginseng, chestnuts, and sweet potatoes.

8. Make the sauce by mixing all the sauce ingredients together.

9. After rice is finished cooking, put rice on a sheet of seaweed and drizzle with sauce.

10. Roll the rice up in the seaweed like a roll cake.

11. Decorate with flowers.

GRANDMA Z'S BROWNIES

BY Abby Wiegers

My mother is shouting, asking for the score of the game. No one can hear her. The warm-blooded, busy-bodied living room—full of uncles, aunts, cousins, and grandparents—seems calm compared to the utter disarray of the kitchen. An audible, resigned sigh escapes her lips as she returns to her work. She has been double-checking the recipe for "Grandma Z's Brownies" from a slip of paper, squinting as she goes, yet refusing to put on her glasses. She knows the recipe by heart—we all do—yet she checks anyway. A simple flour or salt mistake would be recognized quickly by all the traditionalists in the home who like their football on Sundays and their brownies just right. The recipe has been written and rewritten countless times. No one is sure where the original copy lies. Yet somehow, in ways unknown to me, the recipe is constant.

Fall winds through my hometown, bringing with it a cool, crisp breeze. Upon opening the door to my house, however, I am greeted with a wall of warmth that envelops me and carries my feet toward its source—the brownies. The living room is booming with company, partly because family and friends are important in my family, and partly because Sunday night football is a close second.

Perhaps it had been a stressful day. Perhaps work had

been long for some and perhaps patience had been short. Whatever the case, no one can remember it now, because the television is too loud and everyone is yelling about the game, and, "When will the brownies be done?" It feels as though I have been waiting for these delicacies for ages, though I only walked through the door a short while ago.

Mom opens the oven in the burgundy, outdated kitchen. It is the only appliance in the home that has not yet needed to be replaced. Maybe, deep down, we just do not want to replace it for fear of having to learn how to bake brownies in an efficient oven. When it opens, the sound of the pan hitting the metal inside seems to settle the suspense. Everyone is aware that in thirty minutes, my mom will be asking who wants vanilla bean ice cream atop their brownie and who will be "missing out" on such a warm and cool concoction. She begins, now, to make the frosting. Ingredients are added here and there—a little butter, a lot of sugar, and a heap of chocolate chips.

Mom turns to me, face red with accomplishment. "Brownies make even this bad game better," she says. It is then that my ears tune in to the living room conversation once again. Grandpa is retelling the stories of when they would watch wrestling on Sunday afternoons while my great grandma baked Grandma Z's Brownies. He is interrupted by Uncle Dan, who has a tale to tell about those grandparents and the old barns on their property that nearly went up in flames at his childhood hands. His brother chimes in, "Hey, at least we were not as wild of children as Great Uncle Kenny and Great Uncle Larry." They always seemed to find themselves in trouble with folks at the boat launch. I have heard these stories so many times it is as though I remember being there, too.

Our football team is losing, but now no one is

shouting. The oven timer goes off, echoing throughout the house. Mom spreads the frosting across the top of the brownies so richly that not a bite is left uncovered. The knife sinks into clean lines across the pan, and my sister exclaims that the middle piece is hers. No one minds. A Grandma Z's Brownie is just right, no matter where in the pan it lies. I select an edge piece and a scoop of ice cream is mounted on it, instantly melting when it meets the brownie. I admire its deep color, almost visibly seeing the calories it contains. I look around as everyone dives in at the same time, eyes lighting up with pleasure. Smacking sounds consume the room. The brownie hits my tongue all at once, and my tongue explodes. Moist brownie bits stick to the roof of my mouth. The frosting lavishes its warmth on my tongue. I tell myself that I only should have one, yet I find my hand reaching for the pan and digging out a second. Everyone does. Within minutes, all the effort of my mother has been diminished into a thousand crumbs on the table floating in pools of melted vanilla ice cream.

I settle back and begin to realize that my family is represented in this moment. We are made from scratch— pinches of memories and tidbits of stories all mixed and blended together. Love holds us all in one and coats us richly. We are messy and busy like the table and the sounds from the television in the nearby room. Young and old, we reflect the recipe with stained, sloppy handwriting from my great, great grandmother.

Tomorrow will be chilly, as today was. Tomorrow, there will be no football, no loud conversation, and no brownies. There will only be this memory. Perhaps this story will be told at the next gathering, adding to the long list of history that makes us who we are. Tomorrow, my home may not be as warm, but my heart will be full—so will my belly—with Grandma Z's Brownies.

. . .

GRANDMA Z'S BROWNIES

INGREDIENTS

2 cups sugar

1 cup margarine

1 tsp vanilla

½ tsp salt

4 eggs

DIRECTIONS (BROWNIES)

1. Mix ingredients together and add:
2. ½ cup milk
3. 1½ cups flour
4. 4 squares bakers chocolate
5. Heat in oven at 350°F for 30 minutes.

DIRECTIONS (FROSTING)

1. 1 cup sugar
2. ¼ cup butter
3. ¼ cup milk
4. 1 cup chocolate chips
5. Heat on stove until boiling.

KUGELIS: LITHUANIAN POTATO PUDDING

BY **Brittany Dole**

The table will be set for Thanksgiving at the Dole residence. All eyes will be on the kitchen. I envision my mom standing by the oven in her nice holiday clothes. Christmas music will be playing in the background. In fact, I can perfectly hear Mariah Carey's rendition of "O Holy Night" in my head right now. If that caught you by surprise—yes, my family listens to Christmas music on Thanksgiving. It goes hand in hand with the food tradition.

Kugelis is the main attraction of Thanksgiving dinner, and it's *kugelis* that my mom will be working on while everybody else waits expectantly. That doesn't mean we don't appreciate and devour green bean casserole and stuffing and all the rest. It means my family is part Lithuanian. My great-great-great grandmother from Lithuania was the first one to make *kugelis*, but it's stuck for 75 years due to its popularity amongst family members. Its preparation usually falls to the oldest female of the household.

If you were at my house, in addition to the background Christmas music you would hear my mom painfully grating eight pounds of potatoes to feed my large family. Even with help from others, it's extremely tiring to hand-grate potatoes. It makes a slushy and slightly uncomfortable sound as the potato goes across the edged blades. This dish takes a lot of effort and strength to prepare—that's why many Lithuanians only have this dish on holidays. That's a major problem for those of us who don't have the talent to master this art, but wouldn't mind having it as part of our daily diet.

Once my mom adds milk, diced onions, bacon and eggs to her pan, she puts it straight into the oven. It takes about five minutes to smell the sweet aroma of fried bacon and onions sizzling in the pan prior to joining the potato mix. At this point, I begin to notice the delicious scent spreading into every square inch of the house. Some family members lingering in the kitchen will ask, "How much longer?" The scent, if not the food itself, usually sticks around through the next morning. I remember that element the most as a child. I always wondered if it was weird to look forward to waking up the next day to the smell of *kugelis*. Fact is, now that I'm older I really don't care if it's weird or not.

Now the food will be ready and most of the dinner guests will start their plate off with a piece of the long-awaited *kugelis*, topped with a dollop of sour cream. Turkey, green bean casserole, cranberries, stuffing, corn, and *kugelis* make a perfect combination. I always go back for seconds—okay, thirds. As with many other families, food is a major part of my family tradition. It brings us together, but also gives happiness and comfort. The really neat thing is that this dish made generations before me happy too, all the way back to Lithuania. The first time I tried it, I actually hesitated before taking that first bite. It didn't look appetizing to me at the young age of 4, but I'm sure glad I gave it a whirl.

Each year when my mom prepares *kugelis*, I get small

flashbacks of my childhood. I replay things in my head that my late grandmother, uncle, and grandpa said at or near the dinner table. My grandma would ramble on about Black Friday and how completely silly the whole concept seemed to her. As for my grandpa, all he cared about was football and food. Maybe that is where I inherited my love for the sport. My uncle would happily hum along to the Christmas tunes. These are sounds I surely miss since they are no longer to be found on Earth. As I get older, I realize more and more the importance of family foods. We do not eat only to survive. Along with our own little spin on a famous Lithuanian dish, laughter, stories, and memories are also served at my family's table. I am grateful for that.

. . .

KUGELIS

INGREDIENTS

8 large baking potatoes, about 5 lbs

1 medium onion

½ lb bacon

1 cup milk

3 eggs, beaten

Salt and pepper

1 Tbsp flour

2 tsps baking powder

¼ lb butter

DIRECTIONS

1. Peel and coarsely grate the potatoes. Add salt while you grate them.

2. Grate the onion with the potatoes and set aside.

3. Slice bacon into small slices and cook bacon slowly on a medium heat until brown.

4. Add butter to bacon and let it melt. Put that aside.

5. Whip the eggs and milk in a blender until light and fluffy. Add the egg mixture, bacon and butter, flour and baking powder to the grated potatoes mix.

6. Butter a Pyrex baking dish and preheat oven to 400°F. Bake dish for 15 minutes. Reduce to 375°F and bake for 45 minutes or until dish is brown.

7. Let it sit for **15 minutes** while it cools. Serve with a dollop of sour cream.

CHRISTMAS COOKIES
BY Alyssa Mulligan

I wake up every day at the same time. I get out of bed, eat breakfast, and get ready for school. Today, however, is Cookie Day. Cookie Day is the one day out of the entire year that I don't have to be sick to skip school. Every year, on a Wednesday in December, my entire family and I go to my grandma's house to bake Christmas cookies. All of the kids skip school, and all of the adults take off work because we all know that cookies are far more important. My mom, brother, sister, and I all get up bright and early and stuff the car with everything we could possibly need to make our delicious cookies. We head over to my grandma's house. You can practically feel the excitement buzz through the air. Cookie Day is a time where cousins play together, adults gossip, and we all come together to make heaps of cookies to take home to our families. In my opinion, it is the best day of the year.

Once we arrive, my siblings and I sprint into the house to greet our cousins, and of course, we get scolded for not helping our mom carry in all of the ingredients. For a while, once we first get there, we all just sit and talk like we haven't seen one another in ages, even though we only live fifteen minutes away from each other. All of us kids are impatient to start the baking, though, because we know our parents can just talk for hours. However, I often liked to listen to them talk and joke. My family is hilarious. I always look forward to the times when we can all get together and laugh and have fun as a family. After we get reacquainted, it's finally time to bake.

We all cram into my grandma's tiny kitchen. Once the oven starts going, we all begin sweating because of how hot it gets in that stuffy room. Even with the heat, we know it's worth it once we smell the ambrosial scent of the browning cookies. All of my cousins and I keep getting in our parents' way as we try our best to help mix the ingredients together, spoon out the mushy cookie dough, and plop it onto the baking sheets.

We bake so many types of cookies that it usually takes almost the whole day. We make chocolate chip cookies, double chocolate chip, snickerdoodle, peanut butter, oatmeal raisin (which I don't like very much), and many more. Even with this mountain of variety, my cousins and my favorite type to make is sugar cookies because we get to use cookie cutters to formulate the dough into snowmen, Christmas trees, stockings, candy canes, and many more festive shapes. Also, these are the only cookies that we get to decorate with frosting and sprinkles. Before all of that, we mix together butter and granulated sugar until it's light and fluffy. Then, we stir in the egg, flour, baking powder, salt, and vanilla. After that, the cookies are ready to be formed into balls and rolled into more granulated sugar or cut out into the shape of the holiday cookie cutters. Then we put them into the oven and watch them bake.

The only time we take a break is to eat lunch. Every year, our parents go to a Chinese restaurant called Fortune House and get to-go boxes for everyone to share back at my grandma's house. For some reason, my family agreed that Chinese food and cookies are a delicious combination. During this time, we get to relax from our hard work in the kitchen and enjoy greasy, savory Chinese food. After lunch, it's back to baking.

At this point, the whole kitchen and dining room are covered in racks where some of our cookies sit to cool. While those are cooling, we continue baking even more cookies because these have to go around our entire enormous family. It doesn't end there either. We make things besides cookies as well, like coconut macaroons, made with coconut and sweetened condensed milk. Also, there are turtles, assembled from pretzels, Rolos, and pecans, or finally Oreo balls, where you mix Oreo pieces and cream cheese together and douse that combination in a delicious pool of melted chocolate. After all the baking and cooling is done it's time for the adults' least favorite activity: cleanup.

On the other hand, it's the time the kids have been waiting for: decorating. We pull out our tubes of icing and bottles of Christmas sprinkles as our parents remind us, "The icing goes on the cookies, not just into your mouths!" However, we never truly pay any attention to that warning. We have a lot of fun decorating the sugar cookies even though we are all terrible artists. We also try to sneak a few cookies for ourselves while our parents aren't looking, up to the point where we are completely stuffed and can't eat another bite. By the end, everything is a terrible mess but we all had so much fun that it does not matter. Cookie Day is a special day for my family because it is a yearly tradition, unique to us.

Cookies take precedence over everything else for just one day out of the whole year. On this day, we get to leave all of our worries and stress at the door and just be together as a family while creating something incredibly delicious.

• • •

SUGAR COOKIES

INGREDIENTS

1 cup (2 sticks) butter, softened

1 ½ cups granulated sugar

1 egg

2 ¼ cups all-purpose flour

½ tsp baking powder

½ tsp salt

1 tsp vanilla

¼ cup granulated sugar for rolling cookies

DIRECTIONS

1. Preheat oven to 350°F. Line cookie sheets with parchment paper or a nonstick baking mat.

2. Cream together butter and granulated sugar until light and fluffy, about 3 minutes. Add egg and mix until well-combined.

3. Stir in flour, baking powder, salt, and vanilla.

4. Scoop cookie dough by the tablespoon and roll into ball

5. Add granulated sugar to a large bowl for rolling cookie dough in before baking. Place each ball of cookie dough into the bowl of granulated sugar and roll to coat well. Place cookie dough onto baking sheet, spacing about 1 ½ to 2 inches apart. Lightly press each cookie down. Bake for 8 to 10 minutes or until lightly browned.

A SAFE HAVEN IN THE LAND OF KALE & JUICE CLEANSES

BY Aubrey Weedman

I come from a bloodline of quick wit and take-out dinners; fast is a notion we can get behind. But on Thanksgiving, this easy-going family of mine spends a little more time crafting a menu to devour in between bits of conversation. On this day, we take our time with each delectable bite, enjoying the company of those we love and laugh with the most. Plus, by pacing ourselves, the buttons of our best jeans do not come flying off as we get up to grab a heaping second helping from the endless options of hot dishes available. Each of the three families who come together as one at my Aunt Tricia and Uncle Jeff's house takes a part of the menu on as their own to cook (or buy, seeing as King's Hawaiian and Ocean Spray do not freely advertise their recipes for soft dinner rolls and jellied cranberry sauce) before making the trek to Mission Viejo, California. My family lives the farthest away of the three—a whole twenty-minutes and two major streets away.

Before we can go savor my uncle's perfectly browned turkey—which is cooked every year with a method derived from some sort of tip from Food Network star Alton Brown—my immediate family has to contribute their portion of the anticipated feast. Usually, this task falls on my dad, who is the cook in my otherwise culinary-challenged house. Ironically, my dad—a Weedman—specializes in mashing the potatoes made famous by Wahlstroms. To start the process, he artfully peels the russet potatoes in our scratched ceramic sink and boils the starchy chunks in a big black pot. The stewpot reminds me a little bit of a witch's cauldron, which is appropriate considering the meals that are prepared with it never cease to be anything less than devilishly good. After draining the water, my dad mashes the now tender chunks into a fluffy mound before folding enough butter and sour cream into the dish to put a dairy farm out of business. Once Great Grandma Sather's Potatoes are transferred into a deep casserole dish, baked in the oven to achieve a golden top, and safely zipped into their dark green Pyrex warming home, my parents, brother, and I pile into our white Volvo and head over to join the rest of my family.

The Weedman clan is notorious for showing up twenty minutes late to every family function so once we finally arrive, we are almost immediately greeted by my Grandma Andy with warm hugs, wet cheek kisses, and a contagious joy that all her "babies" are in one place again. For as long as I can remember, most of my extended family on both sides has lived within 45 minutes of me. The same cannot be said for my grandparents, though, who have moved around a number of times in their decades of marriage. While they've lived in California since my little brother Hunter was born, my grandparents were not here for my own developmental milestones and toddler meltdowns because they had moved back to their homeland, Minnesota, for my grandpa's promotion right before I was born. This decision took a major toll on my grandma, as she was left all alone in a big house a thousand miles away from her first grandbaby while my grandpa traveled most of the week. Knowing this, her bubbling, tangible excitement when the whole family can be together (no matter how close in proximity we are to one another now) is understandable.

Finally together, we dig into our highly anticipated feast. Rarely do we choose to place the dishes on the pale yellow table, instead opting for a buffet-style meal. Kids always get to start the buffet line, like grand marshals leading the highly anticipated Macy's Thanksgiving Day Parade that we end up sleeping through. While I am the oldest of five grandkids, I still capitalize on this juvenile privilege and use my status as the only girl to bully the boys into letting me be the very first to trek down the buffet line. I grab my paper plate and make my way down the stretch of family delicacies: Grandma Sather's mashed potatoes, sweet potato casserole, stuffing, white and dark turkey meat, Ocean Spray cranberry sauce, King's Hawaiian rolls, homemade gravy, and green bean casserole. It is a Midwestern feast laden with calories I'll regret the next morning. It is a safe haven in the land of Kale, juice cleanses, and Paleo diets that have become idols to most of the population in California.

I proudly bear my lifelong California residency to anyone who asks where I'm from (and even to some who do not), but at holidays like this I revel in my mom's Minnesotan roots. A scoop of this and a scoop of that later, I am back at my designated place at the old, scratched table, complete with a pink crystal goblet (for water until I am 21) and a homemade place card—my scrapbook-loving aunt's specialty. Minutes later, I am joined by the rest of my family and we say grace. In recent years, as my faith has been discovered and matured, my family nominates me to pray for the meal, an honor my grandpa is happy to pass onto me. Surrounding this faded dinner table are

22 hands, 11 genuine laughers, and some mix and match chairs. These are 22 hands, 11 genuine laughers, and some mix and match chairs that have completely shaped me into who I am and how I interact with the world around me, whether I knew it until this very moment or not. Born and bred in a place made famous by Orange County housewives, it is unbelievably refreshing to sit back, take the mask of "having it all together" off, and just be for a while—unbuttoned pants and all.

In my 18 years of experience around this oak dining room table, I've come to understand our dinnertime conversations always follow a pattern—a pattern that would be unacceptable at any other table in America. Sparing my audience any gruesome or offensive details, I will simply reveal that this table is where my crude sense of humor took shape. Our family's love language comes in teasing one another. Therefore, anything worthy enough to earn a genuine belly laugh is welcomed at our gatherings. A few jokes and helpings of potatoes later, we all hobble down the three steps that separate the living room from the dining room and pop Elf into the DVD player to kick off the next holiday season: Christmas. We wait for Grandma Andy, Aunt Tricia, and Mom before hitting play; they always like to clean the dishes and divide leftovers between the families right after dinner. I know it would be the right thing to go and help them, but my swollen belly says otherwise. During this waiting period, my cousins hop onto their various tablets, my uncle goes onto his beloved Mac, and my brother and dad turn the football game on. There is little conversation, but it is comfortable. Finally, the ladies from the clean-up crew join us, and we start the night's featured film. As I drift in and out of sleep— no doubt a direct effect of the copious amounts of turkey

I have devoured—I dream of Christmas brunch, when I can feast on my grandma's sticky rolls and egg casserole. As I look around and watch the rest of my family fight a comatose sleep, I know I am not alone.

. . .

GRANDMA SATHER'S SPECIAL POTATOES

INGREDIENTS

8–10 white potatoes, peeled and cooked

1 stick butter

1 pint sour cream

Salt (to taste)

Milk (add to texture)

DIRECTIONS

1. Grease or spray a large round casserole dish.

2. Mash potatoes with all ingredients.

3. Add pats of butter on top and bake uncovered at **350°F** for **30 minutes**.

* Can be refrigerated or frozen for a few days before being baked. From freezer to oven is **350°F** for **1 hour** or more.

DDOK-BOK-GI: SPICY TASTE IN MY MEMORY

BY Jungeun (Jessie) Shin

I was enjoying a moment of silence that rarely happens in my house. Sitting on a comfortable yellow sofa and drinking bitter green tea made me feel like I had become an adult. I had a fashion magazine on hand but instead I was visualizing various sorts of food that my mom might serve for dinner later at night. When I heard a door slamming, I realized that my sweet daydreaming time was over. My sister had arrived back from her elementary school trip. When I went to greet my sister, I caught an unusual scene; she was dragging mom's shirt and begging her to cook something. That was extraordinary because usually we didn't ask our mom to cook certain foods. We knew that she had never been a fan of cooking. However, for the first time, my sister kept pleading with our mom to cook this specific food. In her whining, I could hear the name of the food she wanted. It was *Ddok-Bok-Gi*.

Obviously, by this time I had already tasted *Ddok-Bok-Gi*. It's spicy and a little bit sweet at the same time. It is such a popular dish in Korea that it is impossible to find someone who has never tried it. *Ddok-Bok-Gi* gained popularity after the Korean Conflict, a war between South and North Korea in the 1950s. My sister was one of the few people who had never tried *Ddok-Bok-Gi*, that is, until she went on her school trip. She had a weak tolerance for spicy food and instead always looked for sugary ones. I still don't know how her friend persuaded my sister to eat spicy food, but she finally found another world of spices.

Before the Korean Conflict, flour had been uncommon and expensive, but after the war, American soldiers provided flour with the other aid they sent. From that time on, flour became more popular. Koreans had sampled various rice cakes from the past, but rice was somewhat expensive and always sweet. This time, people made a rice cake out of flour and added traditional Korean red pepper sauce to make it spicy. It was a huge success since it was both unique and spicy, and many Koreans like spicy food. The red pepper sauce was the key factor that brought success to this food, because the sauce was familiar to everyone. Even though the combination with flour was new, red pepper sauce was an honored part of our tradition.

Whenever my family traveled to the rural area where my grandmother lived, we received a huge bowl of red pepper sauce. The longer red pepper sauce ferments, the better it tastes, and my grandmother would ferment it in a crock for a long time. That definitely made the food special.

My sister was still begging. Mom told her to find her *Ddok-Bok-Gi* somewhere else, but she raised her voice and begged for it even louder. It seemed like she wanted the food at that very moment. Mom seemed pretty surprised that my sister didn't give up on asking her. But there is no parent whose will wins out over their children's; in the end, mom wore an apron and went into the kitchen with her phone to look up a recipe. Surprised to see my mom getting ready to cook, I went after her, full of curiosity.

The kitchen was soon filled with the warm smell of

steamed rice cakes, the spicy smell of red pepper sauce, the pungent smell of green onions, and the fresh ocean smell of fish cakes. The first step my mom took was to boil the water with ground anchovies and kelp to make a tastier broth. I asked her why we didn't use plain water. She said that we could use plain water but adding anchovies and kelp creates a broth that tastes a little like meat and vegetables. She told me that most people use an artificial seasoning instead of making it by themselves. She didn't believe that an artificial seasoning was healthy; thus, she didn't want to use it, especially when she was preparing a meal that we were going to eat. I was surprised and excited to see the change in my mom's attitude towards cooking. Mom, who I thought was lazy when it came to cooking, made her own seasoning, which was an additional step before diving into the actual cooking. She looked like a professional cook who would come out of a television. I kept watching her with delight. Mom then put Korean red pepper sauce into the boiling water and stirred constantly. We had the best red pepper sauce ever, thanks to my grandmother.

For the next step, people usually put in spoons of sugar to make it sweet, but my mom instead put in oligo-saccharide to make it healthier and less sweet. She cut the rice and fish cakes into smaller pieces and put them into the soup. She added chopped green onion and sliced boiled eggs last.

I was watching my mom the whole time. It was amazing to see her cooking something new in our kitchen. I could see sweat beading on her forehead and the focus of her eyes as she bent over the food. It was an amazing view! I wanted to cook like her. After she had finished, she asked me to gather everyone into the dining room. I ran into my dad's room, where my sister and dad were watching Korean drama, and the air seemed full of tension. I shouted to my sister that the food was ready, and my sister ran into the dining room. Dad wanted to continue watching the drama, but I pulled him along with me too. My sister quickly jumped up on a chair. She was very excited and pulled herself as close as possible to the food. When everyone gathered around the table, my sister was the first one to begin eating. Her eyes were twinkling. She stood up and hugged mom tightly, but she didn't stop chewing. My mom looked happy to see my sister getting excited about spicy food. I know there was laughter, but it's the smell of the food that my mom made that will remain in my memory for a long time.

• • •

DDOK-BOK-GI
(Steamed Rice Cakes with Red Pepper Sauce)

INGREDIENTS

4 fish cakes, halved (**8** pieces)

500 g rice cakes, steam cooked and cut into proper size

3 Tbsps red pepper sauce

4 Tbsps oligosaccharide

5 cups water

3 anchovies, ground

2 kelps

GARNISH

1 green onion, cut to **1 cm** (**⅖ inch**)

2 eggs, boiled and cut in half

PIZZA BREAD: A TWIST ON AN OLD CLASSIC

BY Colin Stravers

The white, sticky dough sits wrapped in a shroud of clear saran wrap. From the kitchen, my brother screams, "Mom, what's for supper?" After a slight pause, she responds, confirming that we are having pizza bread tonight. Spirits soar, grins arise, and texts are sent to friends reading, "It's pizza bread night. Are you going to be here?"

Pizza is such a cliché favorite food in today's culture. However, my family has both a generational story and a twist on the recipe to back up our love for the original Italian flatbread. It all started on a Saturday back when my father was a kid.

Alternating between loose meat sandwiches and homemade pizza, Saturday supper was something my Dad looked forward to. My Grandma Gladys's style of cooking was like many other grandmothers': without a recipe. Every other week, she made the pizza with a handful of cheese and a bit of sauce and just the right amount of homemade dough. Instead of cups and ounces, there were pinches and handfuls.

Eventually, my Dad's pizza-loving childhood transitioned into a new tradition. Back on a Sunday evening when I was a kid, my brothers, Justin and Ian, and I, all dressed up in our Sunday khaki shorts, would shoot through the door, crash through the kitchen, slip around the corner, and finish our race by vaulting the sofa to land firmly on the living room floor in front of the flat screen. The television would echo exactly what we were thinking: "This is Sunday Night Football." Attending Sunday night church was a regular part of our agenda, but racing home hoping to catch the kickoff was a requirement.

Dad would place the grocery store frozen pizza into the oven during a commercial break. By the end of the first quarter he pulled it from the oven, popping and sizzling, while the sweet aroma of pepperoni and sausage lured each of us from where we had settled. The circular shape of the pie matched our wide eyes. After the mandatory cooling time, my dad would lead the charge by cutting into the pizza with the sharp crack of a knife. Sundays passed, pizzas were consumed, and life went on.

But life eventually changes, and so did the pizza. Throughout the years, it was folded into a calzone, crammed into ravioli-shaped rolls, and even deconstructed and pigeon-holed into a Lunchable tray. I can't tell you when or why she started making this meal, but my Mom decided to make her own version of pizza called pizza bread.

Three. Three hours are required for preparation; three main steps are performed; three loaves are always the yield in the Stravers household, no matter who is home to consume it. Three boys are willing to help just so they can reap the rewards later. It begins in the early afternoon when she sets out the dough to thaw. At around 5:00 PM, she untangles the puffy, sticky dough from its web of saran wrap and lines up each loaf like soldiers along the black countertop.

The way she proportions noodles and sauce in pasta;

the way she knows the perfect time to flip an egg without glancing at the bottom; the way she rolls out the dough to exactly the right dimensions with a few passes of a rolling pin—my mother seems to have an instinct in the kitchen that I can never replicate. When I grasp the rolling pin, it's as if I am wielding a knitting needle. The dough stretches, but as soon as I stop rolling, the white glob returns to its original shape. When I finally achieve the perfect length, the width is sorely disappointing. I need to fight with the stretchy substance for what seems like hours before I finally achieve the appropriate rectangular shape.

Cheese, cooked sausage, pepperoni, and a buttery baste are next. Again, I show my inexperience as I ask, "How much do I put on?" My mom replies softly, "Whatever looks right. Just cover it well." Cooking is sometimes called an art and not a science. The ingredients aren't always measured. It often requires more finesse than logic. We don't measure the cheese by strands and place them into the properly aligned spot. Instead, we throw it onto the canvas of dough like a Jackson Pollock painting.

Next we roll up each rectangle of dough tightly and my mom wraps the ends underneath like the sheets on the end of a bed. She does it with a smoothness that is once again unmatched by my attempts, which result in spilled sausage and holes that provide a looking glass into the interior of the dough. The loaves are slathered in a baste that leaves a familiar aroma in the air. The smell reminds me of summer nights, enjoying pizza bread with friends. It reminds me of nights when the whole family is finally all gathered. It reminds me of the countertop at which I was raised to prepare the food we enjoy. It reminds me of the generations before me that shaped my parents, and the traditions that shaped me.

When the time comes to eat the pizza bread, two competitions begin. The first is to avoid getting the job of cutting the loaves. The cutter labors through each of the three loaves while everyone else grabs pieces as they are cut and stakes their place in front of the television. The second competition is one of consumption. My brothers and I take pieces three at a time and race to finish before going back for seconds. No matter how much we eat, there still seem to be leftovers for days.

It began with my dad's childhood Saturday-night homemade pizza and it ends with my own empty plate and full stomach. This generation of the Stravers sits gathered around the television, breathing in the aroma of pizza bread and exhaling the pleasure of the familiar tradition. Who knows? Eventually each of us kids may be the parent sending a text that reads, "It's pizza bread night. Are you going to be here?"

• • •

PIZZA BREAD

INGREDIENTS (PIZZA BREAD)

3 loaves frozen bread dough, thawed

1 lb meat of choice (sausage, pepperoni, ham)

2–3 cups shredded mozzarella

INGREDIENTS (BUTTER TOPPING)

½ cup margarine, melted

1 tsp oregano

1 tsp garlic salt

1 tsp parsley

DIRECTIONS

1. Approximately **3 hours** prior to eating, roll out each loaf to approximately **9×13-inch** size.
2. Brush with butter topping.
3. Top with meat and cheese of choice.
4. Roll up starting at narrow end. Place seam side down on greased cookie sheet and roll ends under loaf.
5. Brush rolled loaf with remaining butter topping.
6. Let rise for **2 hours**.
7. Bake at **350°F** for **30 minutes**.
8. Serve with pizza sauce.

WE MADE THEM

BY Emily Homman

My family is extended only by my mother's two siblings, and their small families. We always used to rotate holidays. My mother had Thanksgiving, my grandmother: Christmas; my aunt: Valentine's Day and St. Patrick's Day; and finally we would finish the season with Easter back at my grandmother's. Pecan rolls made on Thanksgiving weekend gave us a break from the worries of everyday life and were the armistice call to herald the Christmas season.

In the weeks leading up to Thanksgiving, the kitchen in our big red farmhouse was converted into a war room in which my mother, older sister, and I rigorously planned a feast. Our staging area was a tiny blue kitchen with worn out, stick-on linoleum floor tiles, blue speckled Formica countertops, and old, flower wall paper that used to be white, with an Amish corner table taking up most of the space. My grandmother loved all things Amish. It was quite the place to stage a battle.

Thanksgiving weekend was always my favorite holiday: the warmth that emanated from the stove while I welcomed family inside, the fancy tableware that sat on display, which was only brought out from its residence in the basement once a year for this very occasion, the wood burner in the basement spreading a dry ash smell throughout the house, all the while battling back the soon-to-be-winter air. There is something special about the air in fall—how crisp it is, how refreshing it is, even with all of the heavy scents; even with all of the heavy memories. The best memories from Thanksgiving were made after the meal.

That is when the real festivities begin. Games take the place of the precious dishes and the dinner table is surrounded by Amish tall backed chairs (at least three different models). Folding chairs are brought in from the shed, and the piano bench is placed delicately at the corner of the table. My uncle brings out his guitar, my sister her ukulele, my brother his bass, I my violin, and our big farm house is magically filled with music and laughter. It goes late into the night. Christmas Eve this tradition goes even later into the night. The singing and games occasionally stop so that the family can open gifts, race to grab the last of the pecan rolls off of the powdered sugar covered plate, or to watch the youngest kids put on a show, complete with puppets, poems, songs, and dancing all pulled into a convoluted kid version of Jesus' birth. But regardless, Thanksgiving was always my favorite, because it is the beginning of the happiness; you can anticipate all of the wonderful things to come.

The rest of the weekend is filled with lazy days, goodbyes to relatives, and baking Christmas cookies. Friday is usually filled with cleaning up the battlefield, playing board games, and taking naps, but Saturday... Saturday is the head start to Christmas season. My family didn't put up decorations, we didn't go out to find the perfect tree, and we didn't even play all that much Christmas music; those things were reserved for the week before Christmas. Instead, we made pecan rolls. I don't know if they are Swedish or not, but they always seemed so to me. We still use my great grandmother's recipe today. It's mostly just butter, flour, and powdered sugar. They are crisp, and if you make them right, they melt in your mouth. We made them, rolling the butter and flour into long fingers. We made them, digging out the pecans that grandma got from the Amish store. We made them, as mom recited epic adventures of her family's Swedish Christmas traditions, like Christmas brunch and having to eat dreadfully overcooked korv. We made them, listening to the story of when dad first had dinner with my maternal grandparents, the story always having the food resemble the turkey from National Lampoon's Christmas Vacation. We made them, my dad in the living room with my brother watching movies, both of them periodically coming into the kitchen to steal some of the ones fresh from the oven. We made them, arguing about which Hallmark movies mom wanted us to watch as a family. We made them, my sister turning the radio to classic rock and head banging to the beat while mixing the batter as my mother silently changed the music to lyrical versions of Bible verses, all of us sliding around the kitchen in our socks. We made them, even when we were overcome with the heaviness of this world. We made them.

Last year my grandmother died; four years ago, my grandfather died on Thanksgiving. Our traditions changed after that, but that doesn't mean that Thanksgiving is a sad affair, mostly because last year, the day before Thanksgiving was when my family officially adopted my little sister, after four years of fostering her. My mother still hosts Thanksgiving, but since we moved into my grandparents' old house it feels different—just a bit melancholy. Even though we feel heavy from battle, we still make the pecan rolls. My aunt now hosts Christmas, and we have Easter at the Stockholm Inn to celebrate our Swedish roots. Fresh squeezed orange juice is guzzled, Swedish pancakes are doused in Lingonberry jam, and korv is always on the table. Stockholm Inn is a special place now. When we eat there, we don't think about how much we miss our grandparents; we think about all of the fantastic stories of their lives.

Thanksgiving is no longer a great feast. It is still an event, but no longer a battle. For Christmas we are no longer subjected to dry ham, overdone casserole, and gelatin desserts, no matter how much I wish I could have one more taste. There are still games and music, but it is just a little quieter. The only things that stayed the same are the pecan rolls. We always make them.

• • •

PECAN BALLS

INGREDIENTS

½ **cup** butter, softened

½ **cup** margarine, softened

3 **Tbsps** powdered sugar

2 **cups** flour

1 **tsp** vanilla

1 **cup** chopped pecans

Powdered sugar for rolling

DIRECTIONS

Preheat oven to **300–325°F** and grease a cookie sheet. Mix the first six ingredients by hand until blended, then shape the dough into **1-inch** balls. Place pecan balls on cookie sheet, spacing about 1 inch apart. Bake **45 minutes** or until brown on the bottom. Roll baked pecan balls in powdered sugar.

ACKNOWLEDGEMENTS

As always, it takes a community. Grateful acknowledgement is made to the following, without whom these food essays would not exist, much less be shared:

Nina Mukerjee Furstenau, whose book showed us a way that food essays could also be about family and culture

The Bruce & Mary Leep English Initiative, for giving us the freedom to dream big

Diana Pell, Faculty Secretary, who compiled the essays, communicated with authors, and incorporated revisions

The Trinity Christian College English Department, Alumni Office, and Advancement team

Nicole Saint-Victor, Director of Multicultural Engagement

The families and friends of these authors, who provided the experiences as well as the recipes

The authors, who went far beyond the requirements of the classroom in interviewing family members and friends, retrieving recipes, and crafting and revising these stories for a broader public

You, dear reader, for whom we hope these essays are both entertaining and instructive.

Publishing for Community

APPENDIX

Getting to Know Us: The Story of Our Foods

Inspired by resources such as the Firefox Books, Nina Mukerjee Furstenau's food essays that turn into cultural histories, food narratives from Homer and the Bible, essays from Culture Is Not Optional, Christine Pohl's *Making Room: Recovering Hospitality as a Christian Tradition*, quotations from Henri Nouwen, and the emphasis on diversity in the First Year Forum, we have hypothesized a collection of food essays that would provide an interesting snapshot of the cultural diversity in our classroom.

Here's our task.

Purpose: Explain a recipe but also explore the history—the people, the culture, its foods—that comes to you through it. What are the hands and the interests that left their mark on the recipe or the memories it instigated?

Audience: 250 friends of the college who, we hope, might be sent a copy of this gustatory celebration of our increasingly diverse community.

Guidelines: Make it be interesting, vivid, enjoyable, perhaps also meditative. We're talking about the basics of life, not only biologically speaking but also culturally speaking. At the same time, include the recipe as a real-life artifact and make sure someone who doesn't know your family could actually follow it and imagine how it worked in your life.

Let your reading of Furstenau's *Biting through the Skin: An Indian Kitchen in America's Heartland* guide you. Read like a writer. Look at the way she opens her first paragraphs; the moves she makes out from a specific food and its occasion to a larger context, and then back in again; her sketches of the people involved; her endings; the transition to the recipe, etc. Also trust there's a reason for our being born into the histories we were born into. Our human task, French Huguenot philosopher Paul Ricoeur once said, is to increase our understanding of that history. Our Christian calling, we could add, is to bump it towards a greater faithfulness.

Technical Guidelines: Give your essay a title. Use 4–5 double-spaced pages. Fit in your recipe.

www.ingramcontent.com/pod-product-compliance
Lightning Source LLC
LaVergne TN
LVHW041220080426
835508LV00011B/1019